W. SOMERSET MAUGHAM

A Study of the Short Fiction

Also available in Twayne's Studies in Short Fiction Series

Sherwood Anderson: A Study of the Short Fiction by Robert Allen Papinchak

Donald Barthelme: A Study of the Short Fiction by Barbara L. Roe

Samuel Beckett: A Study of the Short Fiction by Robert Cochran

Jorge Luis Borges: A Study of the Short Fiction by Naomi Lindstrom

Elizabeth Bowen: A Study of the Short Fiction by Phyllis Lassner

Kay Boyle: A Study of the Short Fiction by Elizabeth S. Bell

Truman Capote: A Study of the Short Fiction by Helen S. Garson

Raymond Carver: A Study of the Short Fiction by Ewing Campbell

Willa Cather: A Study of the Short Fiction by Loretta Wasserman

John Cheever: A Study of the Short Fiction by James O'Hara

Robert Coover: A Study of the Short Fiction by Thomas E. Kennedy

Stephen Crane: A Study of the Short Fiction by Chester L. Wolford

Andre Dubus: A Study of the Short Fiction by Thomas E. Kennedy

F. Scott Fitzgerald: A Study of the Short Fiction by John Kuehl

Gabriel Garcia Marquez: A Study of the Short Fiction by Harley D. Oberhelman

John Gardner: A Study of the Short Fiction by Jeff Henderson

William Goyen: A Study of the Short Fiction by Reginald Gibbons

Graham Greene: A Study of the Short Fiction by Richard Kelly

Ernest Hemingway: A Study of the Short Fiction by Joseph M. Flora

Henry James: A Study of the Short Fiction by Richard A. Hocks

Franz Kafka: A Study of the Short Fiction by Allen Thiher

Bernard Malamud: A Study of the Short Fiction by Robert Solotaroff

Katherine Mansfield: A Study of the Short Fiction by J. F. Kobler

Flannery O'Connor: A Study of the Short Fiction by Suzanne Morrow Paulson

Liam O'Flaherty: A Study of the Short Fiction by James M. Cahalan

Grace Paley: A Study of the Short Fiction by Neil D. Isaacs

Edgar Allan Poe: A Study of the Short Fiction by Charles E. May

V. S. Pritchett: A Study of the Short Fiction by John J. Stinson

J. D. Salinger: A Study of the Short Fiction by John Wenke

William Saroyan: A Study of the Short Fiction by Edward Halsey Foster

Irwin Shaw: A Study of the Short Fiction by James R. Giles

Isaac Bashevis Singer: A Study of the Short Fiction by Edward Alexander

John Steinbeck: A Study of the Short Fiction by R. S. Hughes

Peter Taylor: A Study of the Short Fiction by James Curry Robison

Robert Penn Warren: A Study of the Short Fiction by Joseph R. Millichap

Edith Wharton: A Study of the Short Fiction by Barbara A. White

Tennessee Williams: A Study of the Short Fiction by Dennis Vannatta

William Carlos Williams: A Study of the Short Fiction by Robert Gish

Virginia Woolf: A Study of the Short Fiction by Dean Baldwin

Twayne's Studies in Short Fiction

Gordon Weaver, General Editor
Oklahoma State University

W. Somerset Maugham
Courtesy Popperfoto

W. SOMERSET MAUGHAM

A Study of the Short Fiction

Stanley Archer
Texas A&M University

TWAYNE PUBLISHERS · _NEW YORK_
Maxwell Macmillan Canada · _Toronto_
Maxwell Macmillan International · _New York Oxford Singapore Sydney_

Twayne's Studies in Short Fiction Series, No. 44

Copyright © 1993 by Twayne Publishers

Twayne Publishers
Macmillan Publishing Company
866 Third Avenue
New York, New York 10022

Maxwell Macmillan Canada, Inc.
1200 Eglinton Avenue East
Suite 200
Don Mills, Ontario M3C 3N1

Library of Congress Cataloging-in-Publication Data

Archer, Stanley.
  W. Somerset Maugham : a study of the short fiction / Stanley Archer.
     p.   cm. — (Twayne's studies in short fiction ; no. 44)
  Includes bibliographical references and index.
  ISBN 0-8057-0856-1
  1. Maugham, W. Somerset (William Somerset), 1874–1965—Criticism and interpretation.   2. Short story.   I. Title.   II. Series.
PR6025.A86Z552   1993
823'.912—dc20   92-42071
                                                                             CIP

The paper used in this publication meets the minimum requirements of American National Standard for Information Sciences—Permanence of Paper for Printed Library Materials. ANSI Z3948-1984. ⊚™

10 9 8 7 6 5 4 3 2 1

Printed in the United States of America

For Kerstin, Bill, and Randy

Contents

Preface

W. Somerset Maugham (1874–1965), one of the most popular writers who ever lived, produced well over 100 short stories during an amazingly varied literary career that spanned more than a half-century. A licensed physician who set himself the goal of becoming a professional writer, he succeeded beyond anything he could have expected. Yet his astonishing popularity and success, along with his tendency to deprecate his stories as commercial, combined to produce a largely negative reaction from serious critics. Only a few professional or academic critics, notably Desmond MacCarthy, Cyril Connolly, and Richard Cordell, took Maugham's short fiction seriously during his lifetime.

During his long career an influential and damaging critical theory gained currency: it averred that despite the literary promise inherent in his early autobiographical novel, *Of Human Bondage* (1915), Maugham's work never again reached its thematic depth or affective character portrayal. Following his death biographies and memoirs clarified Maugham's life in ways that seemed to explain and support the negative critical view. His traumatic childhood and carefully closeted homosexuality were cited as biographical elements that sufficiently explained a lack of emotional depth and serious thematic content. The biographies of Ted Morgan and Robert Lorin Calder, as well as the searching analysis of Maugham's early years by Joseph Dobrinsky, make the essential factual bases for this interpretation plausible. And yet similar factors might be discovered in the lives of authors who handily fit the critical requirements of depth and subtlety, authors like Marcel Proust and E. M. Forster.

In analyzing Maugham's short fiction, I have chosen to center on philosophical and literary influences on his life and career as important factors in his writing. Doubtless, biography had an important role, but Maugham criticism, limited thus far in scope and development, has exaggerated its role. Equally if not more important is the aesthetic tradition that shaped Maugham's attempts to contribute to the literary legacy of his nation. Quite apart from being a master craftsman,

Maugham has a claim as a serious realist whose stories are still readable nearly a half-century after he completed his last one.

In the first section I survey the nine volumes of short fiction Maugham published during his lifetime, with a view toward tracing his development as a storyteller. The book attempts to demonstrate that the first 21 titles, largely neglected heretofore, not only provide sources for later fiction and drama but foreshadow and illuminate important elements of Maugham's narrative art. Additionally, they introduce the usual themes and character types that permeate Maugham's fiction. In analyzing later stories I have centered on narrative art and characterization, while at the same time clarifying Maugham's themes.

Part 2, "The Writer," offers a sampling of Maugham's critical writing about the short story as a genre. The sheer length of Maugham's relevant criticism is daunting; except for those who wrote books on the short story, it would be difficult to name a writer who equaled Maugham's critical output on the genre. Of a piece with his fiction, his criticism follows a traditional approach, expressing insightful views in graceful style. I have attempted to select works that shed the greatest light on Maugham's own creative practice and clarify his values when applied to the works of others.

In view of the limited amount of criticism on the short fiction, for part 3 I have selected essays by eminent younger contemporaries of Maugham and one general essay as examples of representative criticism.

It is impossible to acknowledge all who have contributed to this project, for I am indebted to numerous colleagues from my own university and abroad. It is a pleasure to acknowledge a few whose contributions have been either specific or pervasive. I am indebted to Gordon Weaver, general editor of the Twayne series, for his early encouragement and to Daniel Fallon, dean of liberal arts, Texas A&M University, for supporting the academic leave that enabled me to complete this project. Two colleagues, James F. Peirce and Margaret Ezell, generously offered specific assistance. Richard H. Costa and the late Forrest Burt shared my enthusiasm for Maugham and over number of years shaped my views. Paul Pollak and Peter Henderson of the King's School, Canterbury, made the use of the Maugham Library both convenient and pleasant. My greatest debt is to Mary Lee Archer, a Maugham scholar in her own right, whose assistance has been constant, informed, and generous beyond measure.

Part 1

THE SHORT FICTION

Introduction

Looking back on his long career at age 70, W. Somerset Maugham somberly considered which of his numerous literary works would endure. With more than 30 dramas, 20 novels, 3 travel books, 91 collected short stories, 1 major autobiography, and 4 volumes of critical and miscellaneous essays to his credit, his had been one of the most varied and productive literary careers in history. During a writing career that spanned over more than a half-century, he left only one major literary genre, poetry, untouched. And his success, measured by his worldwide readership and his profits, had rarely been surpassed, even though his first decade of writing had proved discouraging. For a late novel like *Then and Now* (1946), the audience was such that the publishers set an initial press run exceeding 750,000 copies. His biographer estimates that before Maugham's eighty-eighth birthday, his books had sold 40 million copies worldwide.[1] From a single short story, "Rain," his earnings exceeded $1 million, largely derived from its production as a drama and from three movie versions. Millions had read his works, and countless other millions had viewed popular screen and stage adaptations that starred the leading actors and actresses of their day.

For Maugham—the orphaned son of a British solicitor and a man afflicted with a stammer and inordinately shy by nature—life as a writer brought wealth and fame after he had rejected a career as a licensed physician to try his luck with literature. Following his early successes in drama, Maugham bought a house in the fashionable Mayfair district of London and traveled the world. In 1926, he obtained the Villa Mauresque on the French Riviera, where he entertained celebrities and royalty. He acquired an extensive collection of impressionist and modern paintings. He gained access to social circles that as an aspiring, struggling young writer of the late 1890s he could only yearn for.

Like Maugham's major novels, his short stories became known to millions who never read them. Maugham himself adapted "The Letter" as a drama, and it enjoyed success on stage and in subsequent movie versions. The movies *Quartet* (1948), *Trio* (1950), and *Encore* (1951) each brought three or four stories to a large viewing audience. Richard Cordell

3

points out that, beginning in 1960, 63 Maugham stories were turned into weekly televised dramas for the British public.[2] *Ashenden* served as the basis for a 1936 movie and a 1991 television miniseries. Further, stage and screen adaptations of stories like "Rain," "The Letter," "The Vessel of Wrath," and "Lord Mountdrago" were translated and successfully adapted to audiences in France and Germany.

At age 70 Maugham's successes lay behind him, and the hope for fame beyond life became more pressing. He considered that, owing to its length, his most significant novel, *Of Human Bondage* (1915), would not last, even though after 30 years it was still widely read. A handful of plays, highly acclaimed when they were produced in the early decades of the twentieth century, would probably find a place in the history of drama as examples of the comedy of manners. Among them dramas like *The Constant Wife*, *The Circle*, *Mrs. Dot*, *Smith*, and *Our Betters* remain candidates for stage revivals. And finally, perhaps a dozen of his short stories, he thought, would survive for future readers, though he named no titles. "Slender baggage," Maugham ruefully declared, to accompany one into eternity.[3] But perhaps *slender* is appropriate only to a writer of Maugham's astonishing productivity. While the winnowing of time—an indispensable process for all modern fiction—will reveal the accuracy of his assessment, most Maugham critics appear to agree that a handful of short stories will be among his works that survive.

Beginning with *Orientations* (1899) and concluding with *Creatures of Circumstance* (1947), Maugham published nine separate volumes of short fiction. Most stories from each collection had been previously published in magazines like *Punch*, *Hearst's International Magazine*, *Nash's Magazine*, and *Cosmopolitan*, for his normal mode of publication was first to sell a story to a magazine and then to publish it in a collection. When asked by Garson Kanin how many stories he had written, Maugham replied without hesitation, "I know exactly. One hundred and four."[4] Like many of his comments about his life and work, this one is misleading. If one includes the 91 titles Maugham chose for the collected edition, plus the 14 "Ashenden" stories he destroyed in manuscript on the advice of Winston Churchill, the total exceeds Maugham's figure by one.[5] Yet in addition to the collected stories, 21 titles have been unearthed and published in *Seventeen Lost Stories* (1969) and *A Traveller in Romance* (1984).

Further complicating matters for a bibliographer was Maugham's practice of recycling, rearranging, and altering the titles of stories. Three stories from his early period were rewritten and included in the collected edition. "Cousin Amy" became "The Luncheon"; "The Happy Couple" and "A Marriage of Convenience," while retaining their original titles, underwent extensive revision. A fourth, "The Mother," retained its original form. The 16 original stories in *Ashenden* (1928) were conflated into 6 for the collection, with one title, "The Flip of a Coin," omitted entirely. In his list of Maugham's short stories and sketches, Anthony Curtis, following John Brophy's precedent of listing the sketches and stories together, includes 191 titles, and the list is by no means complete. If one includes the titles of sketches from the travel literature, on the grounds that some stories in the collected edition like "Salvatore" and "The Portrait of a Gentleman" are essentially sketches, and adds the short stories believed to have been extant at one time, Maugham wrote well over 200 titles. Yet it is safe to assume that his reputation will rest finally on those 91 titles he selected as a part of his "complete" works.

While the genesis of Maugham's stories is somewhat diverse, he developed his basic themes and methods of narration early, and these changed little over a half-century of short story production. Intellectually, he came early under the influence of the pessimistic philosopher Arthur Schopenhauer and those artists who had also been deeply influenced by him: Richard Wagner, Maugham's favorite composer; Guy de Maupassant, the French master of the short story who had been a guest at the salon of Maugham's mother; and Henrik Ibsen, the realistic dramatist. As a student in Heidelberg, Maugham attended Kuno Fischer's lectures on Schopenhauer and carefully marked selected passages in the German anthology of his works in his possession. Schopenhauer's pessimism fit hand in glove with the subsequent medical training at St. Thomas's Hospital that taught Maugham to view human beings with careful clinical detachment and with a tight rein on emotion. Once while dissecting a cadaver, he became incensed that a nerve was not in the normal place. His instructor pointed out to him, "You see, the normal is the rarest thing in the world."[6]

Medical training not only insulated Maugham from emotion and sentimentality; it taught him that careful observation is essential to an understanding of individual uniqueness. For as he observes in *Of Human Bondage*, a human life forms a pattern, and each pattern has unique elements, an idea adopted from Schopenhauer. Unlike the philosopher, who believed that one could recognize the pattern only in retrospect, Maugham in *Of Human Bondage* outlines his belief that an individual can influence the pattern of his or her life. In his autobiography, *The Summing Up*, he professes to have done so with his own. (Maugham never resolved the contradiction between this voluntarism and the determinism of Schopenhauer, which he logically preferred.) Thus his is basically an aesthetic concept of human life that has elements in common with modern existentialism.

Significantly, he observed that in Asia he had met British colonial officials who had patterned their lives after Rudyard Kipling's fictional characters.[7] Not only did he believe this possible; he thought a writer who could exert such influence over human beings merited high praise. He spent much of his literary life sketching the patterns he found in others' lives and exposing the ironic incongruities that simmered beneath the surface. For the pattern, with its subtle incongruities, is discovered only through careful observation. Maugham once confided that he viewed human beings only as the raw material of his work, and elsewhere he remarked that his ideas for stories usually originated with a character that held his attention. Those who met him in society and during his travels came, with disturbing frequency, to recognize themselves in his fiction. John Pollock has shown that despite Maugham's changes of descriptive details, settings, and circumstances, the originals for many characters portrayed in novels, short stories, and dramas were obvious to their contemporaries.[8]

In addition to his pessimism about human life, certain literary influences left their imprint on Maugham's art of fiction. In the 1890s Maugham came under the influence of the aesthetic movement and its chief exponent, Oscar Wilde. During his long literary apprenticeship, he wrote in a wide variety of styles and tried his hand at several genres in an attempt to discover his strengths as a writer. In the novel, for example, he produced a naturalistic work in *Liza of Lambeth* (1897), a historical novel in *The Making of a Saint* (1898), novels of manners in *Mrs. Craddock* (1902) and *The Merry-Go-Round* (1904), and an essentially Gothic novel in *The Magician* (1908).

But he discovered his forte in the comedy-of-manners mode begun in his early dramas and continued in his most successful later dramas. Before its revival by Wilde, the comedy of manners had experienced a long history in English literature, dating back to its flowering during the Restoration. The dramas of Etherege, Wycherley, Dryden, Congreve, and Sheridan found wide acceptance with theater and reading publics. Essentially works of witty, aphoristic repartee and satire, they explore the manners and behavior of adults in a structured, class-conscious society, a society secure enough to laugh at its superficial foibles. The dramas center on sexual mores and are realistic if not cynical in tone.

They accorded well with late-Victorian and Edwardian sensibilities, for the age prized witty diversion and brilliant conversation, punctuated by an abundance of aphorisms and epigrammatic wit. In Maugham's comedies the conflict between the individual and society forms a staple ingredient, often featuring a protagonist who attempts to achieve financial success, secure a niche, or cling precariously to a social level attained through talent or ability. Like the stock characters of the generic tradition, Maugham's have their essential pattern set; they are not developing in any significant way. The crises they encounter are external, and their coping with them does not alter their fundamental being or nature, even though the conflicts they encounter may destroy them. At times Maugham's characterizations, like those of the comedy of manners, teeter on the brink of caricature.

While Maugham's gift for dialogue became apparent before his spectacular success as a dramatist, his playwriting experience left a lasting imprint on his fiction. The fondness for aphorisms, the description of carefully prepared scenes, the natural, colloquial dialogue, and the conflict involving two personalities are repeated throughout the prose narratives. Significantly, in his preface to *Tellers of Tales*, an anthology of 100 short stories, Maugham asserts that a writer must exploit the dramatic elements within a source. The striking dramatic elements in Maugham's stories promote reader involvement with the narration; from a more practical standpoint, they make the stories readily adaptable as dramas.

Maugham's varied achievement and astonishing productivity were in keeping with his conception of literature as a profession. He was motivated by the assumption, widely accepted in European nations from the Renaissance, that professional authors create a nation's literature. He believed that while other countries had produced great writers, only England and France had produced a great literature. But he also embraced a related and more problematic principle: that great writers are recognized during their times. He could point to Shakespeare and Balzac as writers whose works were widely acclaimed by their contemporaries. He perceived but did not accept the fissure that developed during the early twentieth century between the highbrow and the popular artist. To him the lesson of time was clear: that the great writer was also popular and that those writers who appealed only to the elite were soon forgotten. Oddly, he recognized that in painting the great artist is often neglected, even scorned, by contemporaries, but he did not apply this observation to literature. His view led him to reveal a contempt for highbrow critics and for writers whose talents, however brilliant, confined them within a narrow generic range or whose genius appealed only to a limited audience. His commercial successes allowed him to shrug off critical barbs from the elite, though he did not always refrain from repaying his critics with sardonic barbs of his own.

In essence a Maugham story is an exposé of a human incongruity or interesting trait that exists within the pattern of an ordinary human life. The exceptional is to be found everywhere, and Maugham in his voluminous critical writings on the art of the short story likes to stress the anecdotal origins of his stories. From a bare anecdote he perhaps has heard or overheard on his travels, he constructs a complete story. More often he builds a story around a character whom he finds interesting. If no anecdote is available, the story may take another literary work as a point of departure. It is difficult to believe that "The Outstation" could have been written without the earlier example of Joseph Conrad's "An Outpost of Progress" or that plots for "Mr. Know-All" and "A String of Beads" were not really inspired by Maupassant's "The Necklace." A few of the stories are based on Maugham's own experience, notably those in *Ashenden*, inspired by his intelligence work during World War I. Others consist of brief descriptive sketches based on places he has visited or characters he has observed. A few stories are allegorical or moral fables, and a few others explore the occult and abnormal psychology. Maugham's favorite type of narrative, the exotic story, portrays the lives of Europeans or Americans in an alien environment. His best-known stories of this type are set in Malaya, where British nationals struggle against the climate, a foreign culture, and loneliness.

As he attempted to make a life a pattern, Maugham insisted that literary art should reflect the concept of a pattern. Among his canons of criticism, it is hardly possible to exaggerate the importance of this one. When Garson Kanin once suggested, long after Maugham had abandoned the stage, that he write additional plays, he replied that he no longer retained the form of a drama in his head. It is as though one masters a framework, and all else amounts to elaboration.

In the introduction to *Tellers of Tales* (1939), Maugham defines the short story in traditional terms: "I should define a short story as a piece of fiction that has unity of impression and that can be read at a single sitting."[9] In his later essay "The Short Story," he expands the definition somewhat yet retains the concept of the genre as Poe first described it: "it is a piece of fiction, dealing with a single incident, material or spiritual, that can be read at a sitting; it is original, it must sparkle, excite or impress; and it must have unity of effect or impression. It should move in an even line from its exposition to its close."[10] He insists that a short story must have beginning, middle, and end, and that it should move toward its determined end in a linear fashion. Everything contributes to the conclusion, which should not be expected but in retrospect should seem inevitable. Maugham compared his narrative with that of an ancient teller of tales around a campfire and saw no need to change the original narrative technique. He scoffed at the writer who told him he had written a story and was revising it to add subtlety, for Maugham could discover no reason a narrative should involve subtlety. Yet an examination of his stories reveals that his own narrative techniques are not always so simple and straightforward as he claims.

His canons of criticism also included simplicity of diction and style. He was fond of pointing out that the greatest philosophical ideas, those of Hume, Kant, and Schopenhauer, were expressed in pellucid, graceful prose. He observed that if a philosopher could get his ideas across in clear prose, there was no reason a storyteller should not. In a disciplined effort to improve his style, he studied and imitated the prose of Swift, and he expressed his admiration for the styles of Dryden and Tillotson. With few exceptions—his description of Angor Wat being a notable one—he avoided ornateness and profusion. "Simplicity, lucidity, and euphony" represented his ideal stylistic qualities, and in large measure he attained them.

Yet within Maugham's carefully chosen standards, one discovers a great deal of variation. In narrative technique he makes frequent use of the third-person-omniscient narrator, though in the later stories this technique shades smoothly, almost imperceptibly, into a character's point of view. To a remarkable degree he advances his plots through dialogues between two characters, as in drama, and thus one finds an unusual number of dinner meetings in the stories, where he makes the most of his natural gift for dialogue. Often in both the novels and the stories, he invents a character who serves as the author's spokesman, a *raisonneur* like Dr. Macphail in "Rain" who inclines the audience toward the proper perspective.

But by far the most pervasive narrative technique is the use of the Maugham persona, the character who witnesses the action, often first-hand, or hears the narrative from a person he meets. This speaking voice from both the novels and the short stories is that of an author, at first unnamed. In the later prose fiction, he becomes a minor character named Ashenden, or Willie Ashenden, or, in *The Razor's Edge*, "Mr. Maugham." He is an urbane, worldly-wise traveler who keenly observes what others might miss and directs the reader's attention to something significant. He may appear in Seoul, Yokohama, Singapore, Petrograd, Rome, Paris, or New York, or on shipboard bound for a distant port. He reveals little of himself and exerts little influence on the action, but he establishes a friendly relationship with the reader, who enjoys the seemingly candid comments of a successful author. He is skeptical, clinical, and keenly observant of human beings. Free of illusions and ideals, he is often cynical and ironic. He finds rogues and scoundrels more interesting than solid citizens, and his tolerance causes him to try to understand rather than condemn human vices. Although he admires goodness when he sees it, he finds it less interesting to recount than eccentricity, wickedness, and vice. On occasion his reporting is clearly autobiographical, but more often it is mingled with fiction or completely fictional. There is reason to suppose that Maugham himself sometimes blurred the line between fiction and fact, for he was known to introduce himself as "Willie Ashenden" on occasion. Like Hemingway's heroes, the persona is approximately the age of the author at the time of composition, and readers of Maugham can observe the persona changing with age.

Often on his travels the persona meets another character with a story to tell and, after introducing him at the outset, withdraws and lets the character narrate his story. As in the stories of Joseph Conrad, the persona may intervene with a brief comment or question during the narrative or he may resume a dialogue at the end, but he usually remains in the background. The Maugham persona's identity as a traveler only increases his usual reticence and detachment; it places him in the position of an observer reluctant to intervene. The format creates the impression that the reader is hearing the story as the narrator first hears it.

No artist better demonstrates the principle that art exists on the edges or margins. Maugham's characters are often those found just on the outside of society or in an exotic setting. He believed that characters in a modern urban society were eventually worn smooth, as pebbles in a stream are smoothed by constant interaction with water and sand. Those outside society or on its fringes have an opportunity to develop their individualism, to cling to and even increase the kinks in their characters. Maugham sought them early in Malaya but later came to recognize that people all about him showed incongruities that removed them from the ordinary, that the normal was indeed the exceptional.

Orientations and Early Stories

From the beginning of his career in the mid-1890s through 1909, Somerset Maugham wrote and published 21 stories. After 1909, 11 years passed before he published another, for during this period he focused primarily on playwriting and on his autobiographical novel, *Of Human Bondage*. According to his account, two stories from his early period, "Daisy" and "A Sad Case," were written when he was 18 and may well have been the earliest of his extant works. They were submitted for publication to T. Fisher Unwin in 1896, when Maugham was 22, and were rejected, though he included them in the first collected book of stories, *Orientations*. The initial reader, Edward Garnett, suggested by way of encouragement that he submit something longer. In response Maugham produced his first successful work, *Liza of Lambeth*, a naturalistic novel of life in a London slum. To Maugham all the early stories represented insignificant and sometimes embarrassing attempts at prose fiction; except for three that he completely rewrote and one, "The Mother," later published with little alteration, he excluded them from the standard edition of his works, deeming them too immature. In 1935 he wrote of *Orientations*, "I read it again the other day. It sent so many cold shivers down my spine that I thought I must be going to have another attack of malaria."[11]

Yet in retrospect the strictures may have been somewhat severe. According to Karl Pfeiffer, who searched for uncollected early stories during Maugham's lifetime, he located "The Happy Couple" in *Cassell's Magazine* and mailed a copy to Maugham. Although he had completely forgotten the story, Maugham found it promising and rewrote it for *Cosmopolitans*.[12] Anonymous reviewers for the *Athenaeum* and the *Academy* considered *Orientations* superior to his two previously published novels, *Liza of Lambeth* and *The Making of a Saint*. The *Academy* reviewer spotted the resemblance to Guy de Maupassant and praised Maugham's combination of modernism with humor. Maugham later confirmed the Maupassant debt, acknowledging in the preface to *East and West* that before age 18 he had read all Maupassant's good stories.

These early efforts reflect Maugham's fundamental themes and val-

ues, and while the 11-year break between them and "Rain" is significant, it is not so great as Maugham suggests. Their settings, for example,
are the familiar ones of Maugham's later fiction: exotic places like Spain,
France, and Germany; the fashionable London drawing room; the provincial village; the English country house. One also encounters a generous cross-section of Maugham characters—the snob, the scoundrel, the
adventurer, the inveterate traveler, the predatory female, the crashing
bore, the fallen woman who recovers, the self-centered professional
clergyman, and the lawyer. But perhaps the stories are more interesting
to the student of Maugham for what they reveal about his narrative art.

Among those included in *Orientations*, "The Punctiliousness of Don
Sebastian" was Maugham's first in print, having been published as
"Don Sebastian" in the October 1898 issue of *Cosmopolis*, an obscure
magazine that ceased publication before he was paid for his contribution.
Set in Spain, the narrative was inspired by Maugham's trip there in 1897.
It describes Xiormonez, a remote fictional town in Castile, where the
narrator stops to visit a cathedral that houses an ornate Renaissance
chapel of the Losas family and claims to possess the eyebrows of Joseph
of Arimathea. Noting evidence of extreme religious devotion on his
arrival, the narrator encounters the current duke of Losas, an impoverished nobleman who for a franc conducts tourists through his family
chapel.

As the duke comments on the tombs of his ancestors, he hints of a
family scandal chronicled in a manuscript in his possession. Purchased
by the narrator at a bargain, the manuscript reveals a story of adultery,
revenge, and fratricide involving Don Sebastian, an earlier duke; Doña
Sodina, his duchess; and Cardinal Pablo, the duke's brother, a resplen-
dent prelate not known for self-denial. Renaissance splendor as described in the manuscript contrasts sharply with the impoverished
austerity the narrator has observed in the town. After the unexpected
death of his duchess, Don Sebastian discovers incriminating notes in her
breviary written in the hands of his brother and his wife. Convinced of
their import, he says nothing but persuades the cardinal to dine with him
on the anniversary of his wife's death. Wine poisoned by belladonna is
the instrument of the duke's revenge. After the cardinal's death his
beneficiary the duke builds him an elaborate tomb. Later he increases
his fortune through marriage to the wealthiest woman in Spain.

In the final section the current duke joins the narrator at his hotel for
a free dinner. The narrator advises him to repair his family fortune by

marrying an American or British heiress, and offers a letter of introduction to an English heiress of his acquaintance.

From the standpoint of narrative, the story is notable for its frame, a device Maugham exploits to excellent effect later. Though he does not make further use of the lost manuscript convention, he frequently introduces letters and other forms of written messages into later narratives. Generous description of the exotic setting to create an appropriate tone and the dinner where people meet for conversation are staples of Maugham's fiction, as are the themes of infidelity and unpunished crime.

But by far the story's greatest narrative significance lies in its introduction of the Maugham persona, the first-person narrator and observer. Although Maugham employs the first person in *The Making of a Saint*, the novel's narrative voice is a named character. In "Don Sebastian" the speaker is clearly the authorial voice. The principal plot involving the Renaissance duke is narrated in the third person, as if recorded in the manuscript. The frame of the story, the descriptions, and the meeting with the duke are through the eyes of the first person. A sophisticated traveler, a practical realist on the lookout for bargains and interesting, obscure places, he is appreciative of society and its conventions. He has achieved the technique of taking the reader into his confidence, so that the reader shares his angle of vision: "The cathedral is admirable; when you enter you find yourself at once in darkness, and the air is heavy with incense; but, as your eyes become accustomed to the gloom, you see the black forms of penitents."[13] While carefully describing the intensities of religious devotion he has observed, he himself is detached and devoid of illusions. At this early stage the Maugham persona, a cosmopolitan traveler and detached observer who probes for the ironies and incongruities of life, makes his appearance.

The second story, "A Bad Example," draws heavily on the author's experience as a medical student in London. It reflects a favorite Maugham theme—that when idealism and realism clash, idealism must give way. Summoned to duty as a member of a coroner's jury, James Clinton, a complacent, shabbily genteel clerk, witnesses for the first time cases of starvation in a land of abundance and is shaken by the experience. After recovering from a bout of typhoid fever, he asks his wife for a Bible and finds the New Testament passages that impose an obligation to help the poor. Taking the admonitions seriously, he changes his life and begins giving away his resources. As a result, he loses his job and alienates his family. In vain does Mr. Evans, the curate summoned by Clinton's wife, attempt to persuade him that the passages should not be interpreted literally. Finally, a specialist summoned by the family diagnoses "post enteric insanity," and Clinton's family commits him to an asylum.

While the third-person narrative includes lively cockney dialogue, the style is substantially inferior to Maugham's later fluency, relying on too many adverbs and clichés. Yet it offers ironic reversals so often found in the fiction and presents the professional characters, clergy and doctors, as worldly men concerned primarily with their own comforts. The story provided the plot and primary characters for Maugham's final play, *Sheppey* (1933).

In "De Amicitia" a budding English playwright and an American art student travel from Paris to Holland so that she can paint windmills. They plan to maintain their platonic friendship, but as her art teacher had cautioned, their virtuous intentions give way to passion. The story, which has a happy ending, is narrated in the third person, relies heavily on dialogue, and makes extensive use of letters. As in many of the early stories, the episodes are numbered. In the final, brief section, the narrator appears with a new character, his aunt, forming an abbreviated frame that distances the conclusion from the narrative. Their dialogue features the provincial aunt telling him that the two should have got married, and the narrator, flippantly evading the issue, replying, "O, I have no doubt they did" (*Seventeen*, 64).

"Faith," a story of religious conflict, moves adroitly toward its conclusion with neither digressions nor intervention from a narrator. Brother Jasper, a Spanish monk, loses his faith and finds sympathy from an aged prior who is dying of cancer. The prior's successor proves more rigid and less sympathetic. After Jasper has been scourged by the new prior, he recovers his faith through a miraculous vision, only to lose it again when he discovers the vision was an illusion created by sunlight through stained glass. Careful observation has dispelled the illusion and revealed that things are not what they seem. Fleeing the monastery during a snowstorm, Jasper collapses at the foot of a great crucifix standing beside the road and is frozen to death. After several villagers are healed by the touch of his garments, the monks credit him with miraculous power. The themes and characters suggest Dostoyevsky, though the mystical is undercut by irony and realism. Yet in the story Maugham untypically treats the clergy with respect; even the severe new prior is motivated by genuine fanaticism.

"The Choice of Amyntas" introduces a naive young adventurer, son of an impecunious schoolmaster, traveling to seek his fortune in Spain. Choosing an arduous, forbidding course, he travels by boat through a mysterious cavern and emerges into a Moorish paradise inhabited by four beautiful maidens—Power, Riches, Art, and Love. Given his choice, he selects Love, whereupon the others vanish, Power journeying to Germany, Riches to England, and Art trekking the world over in search of patronage. A loosely episodic, highly picaresque narrative, the work satirizes schoolmasters and clergymen, yet it introduces a Maugham character type, the crusty sea captain, a man of experience and, usually, of good will. The allegorical figures represent a departure from Maugham's realism, though he occasionally employs equally fanciful devices in later fiction.

"Daisy," the final selection in the volume, is the rags-to-riches story of a fallen provincial heroine who eventually marries well and becomes a lady. Yet the story's narrative focus is on Blackstable (Maugham's own Whitstable), Daisy's native village in Kent. As the story opens, village gossips spread the news that Daisy Griffith has eloped to London with a cavalry officer stationed in nearby Tercanbury (Canterbury). On Sunday the vicar in his sermon alludes to the scandal, and Daisy's mother and brother persuade her sympathetic but weak-willed father that the family can have nothing further to do with her. After her suitor abandons her in London, they coldly reject her pleas to return home.

Years later Daisy is seen in a pantomime in Tercanbury, playing Dick Whittington, the provincial boy who left his village and became Lord Mayor of London. But the local villagers who recognize her are amazed when Daisy appears wearing diamonds, and the report spreads that she is engaged to Sir Herbert Ously-Farrowham. The village folk who were the first to condemn her now think her family has been far too harsh and un-Christian toward her. They ostracize the family, the father's business fails, and in response to her family's urgent plea for help, Daisy returns for a brief visit. Poised, self-assured, and worldly-wise, she extracts the full truth from her family about their previous treatment of her but refrains from condemning them. Assuring them that her husband will allow them £5 a week, she leaves the village, never to return.

Although the reader sees Daisy only twice—once as a rejected, desperate, almost frantic girl, once as a strong, mature woman—she is one of Maugham's most attractive female characters. With determination, spunk, and perseverance, she triumphs over narrow, conventional villages mores. Yet she retains an endearing vulnerability, as the final scene after her return to her husband indicates. Despite a plot that requires years for completion, Maugham's third-person narrative, laced with heavy-handed irony and satire, is brisk and lively. The villagers' class consciousness and snobbery override their ethical prudishness, exposing it as hypocritical.

Of the 15 stories published in magazines between 1900 and 1909, 9 are set in England, 5 in Europe, and 1 on an island off North Africa. The English settings are richly varied, featuring a fashionable London apartment, a country house, and a village, each capturing a specific social milieu.

Among the 15 stories "Lady Habart" (1900) is the most significant, for its narrative technique illustrates the dramatic possibilities often found in Maugham's fiction. Lady Habart, an unscrupulous London widow who lives beyond her means, is threatened with bankruptcy by one of her creditors, Captain Smithson. The plot develops through five dramatic encounters, closely resembling a five-act structure.

The first, introducing Lady Habart and her feckless brother Guy, provides exposition, for Guy has to report his failure to persuade the captain to delay payment of the debt. The next encounter pits Lady Habart's will and resourcefulness against the adamant Smithson, who rebuffs her charm and hint of favors. Faced with ruin, she receives Ramsden, a former suitor whom she has jilted, and who has arrived at her apartment to denounce her for choosing to marry someone more affluent. Lady Habart acknowledges her guilt and unworthiness, while at the same time professing her undying love of Ramsden, who has recently inherited a fortune of his own. Outwardly unmoved by her tears, Ramsden exits abruptly, only to return the following day to beg her forgiveness, ask her hand, and assume responsibility for her debts. He writes her a check for £4,000, since she has prudently added £1,000 to the £3,000 she owes Smithson.

In the final meeting Smithson appears at her apartment with a new proposal for rescheduling the debt and feels Lady Habart's scorn, contempt, and total triumph. In four successive meetings, each involving intense dramatic conflict, two major reversals are brought about: in the first and fourth, Lady Habart's impending ruin turns to triumph; in the second and third, Ramsden's initial hostility is changed to complete sympathy through her ability as an actress. Maugham used the story as the basis of his first dramatic hit, *Lady Frederick* (1907).

"Cousin Amy" (1908) also centers on character conflict, though its tone is that of light comedy. When the first-person narrator meets his distant cousin in London, she suggests they have dinner at the Ritz.

While talking incessantly about food and diet, Amy, who protests that she eats little, orders the most expensive items—salmon and dishes with resoundingly French names. As successive menu items arrive, the panic-stricken narrator, a writer, wonders whether he can cover the charge. In return for the elaborate meal—topped off by strawberries and whipped cream and a liqueur—Amy invites the narrator to lunch the next day at a vegetarian restaurant. Built entirely around a dinner meeting, the story introduces the first of Maugham's garrulous characters, both male and female, whom the reticent narrator can hardly bear. Amy's successors in the fiction include Max Kelada in "Mr. Know-All" and Miss Reed in "Winter Cruise." For his collected short stories, Maugham revised the story as "The Luncheon," changing the setting and adding a sardonic conclusion.

"Cupid and the Vicar of Swale" (1900), a story of ecclesiastical maneuvering in a village setting, establishes a light Trollopean tone. Maugham reworked the basic plot and characters for his later drama *Loaves and Fishes*. Mr. Branscombe, the newly appointed vicar, becomes engaged to Mrs. Strong, only to learn that she will lose her generous widow's annuity if she remarries. Both a gentleman and an ambitious man, he must extricate himself from his promise in good form. After Mrs. Strong releases him, he immediately announces his engagement to Mrs. Simpson, a widow of assured inheritance, the other village woman considered a suitable match.

In "Pro Patria" (1903) the marriage comedy continues on a slightly more serious note. A dissenting minister has learned that John Porter-Smith, a parliamentary candidate, has been separated from his wife owing to his infidelity. Porter-Smith persuades his wife to rejoin him in denying the story; the minister is satisfied, and after the election the successful candidate and his wife are reconciled.

In "The Happy Couple" (1909) a strong-willed, independent and goodhearted Miss Ley invents a romantic story involving some new neighbors living near her estate in the Thames Valley. Observing their devotion to each other and their infant, she believes them self-sacrificing and idealistic. Her guest, Frank Hurrell, recognizes them as impostors who conspired to murder an old woman for her wealth and escaped a murder conviction only because of insufficient evidence. Aware that they have been recognized, they flee the peaceful valley, thus confirming Hurrell's account. The story reflects Maugham's theme that things are not what they appear and his pervasive tendency to deflate romanticism.

"A Point of Law" (1903) introduces a first-person narrator who consults a solicitor about his will. Mr. Addishaw, the solicitor, then narrates the story of his shrewd move to prevent an adventurer from inheriting the fortune of a dying young woman. The method of narration, with the persona meeting someone with a story to tell, becomes commonplace in Maugham, who employs a similar technique in "Good Manners" (1907). This latter story is set at the country house of Augustus Breton. The protagonist, a wealthy collector, travel writer, and raconteur, was based on Augustus Hare, whose estate Maugham visited and who stressed the importance of manners. After the narrator and a visiting parson are served superb wine at dinner, Augustus recounts the story of its origin. Johann Herz, alias Baron von Bernheim, had moved into the area some years before and ingratiated himself with Augustus through his appreciation of art. After several months of dinners and friendly meetings, Herz was exposed as a swindler and impostor. He took instant flight, only to be apprehended, convicted, and sentenced to a prison term. Augustus bought his remaining store of fine wine at auction but had refrained from drinking any until this dinner, for good manners demand that none of the wine be drunk before the day Herz is released from prison.

"Flirtation" (1906) establishes a comedy-of-manners, war-of-the-sexes tone, with two sophisticates making a game of a wedding proposal. In "The Making of a Millionaire" (1906), a shrewd stockbroker whose speculations jeopardize his clients' security turns the table on his detractors when he receives news of a rich gold discovery and buys back their shares at par before they learn of it.

Of the six stories with exotic settings, three are slight tales indeed. In "A Traveller in Romance" (1909), more a sketch than a story, the narrator travels in winter by coach from St. Moritz to Italy. The narrator reads, as he often does while traveling, and enjoys the Alpine scenery. He is joined in the coach by a commercial traveler who expresses his expansive enthusiasm for Italy as the land of romance. "An Irish Gentleman" (1904) recounts the fanciful adventures, both humorous and harrowing, of a young Irish rogue in Germany. "The Spanish Priest" (1906) develops the theme of lost treasure, an unusual one for Maugham. Yet it, like many of the other early stories, deals with the theme of acquiring money, a subject that concerned Maugham personally during his early years. In Gibraltar the narrator meets a bedraggled mining engineer who recounts his story. A Spanish priest had brought him an ore sample from one of many abandoned mines he explored. Before the test results returned from London, the priest disappeared, and the engineer

began searching for him, since the ore was a rich find. After discovering the priest's maps, he found the priest's body near an abandoned mine, but his lifelong search for the treasure brought him nothing.

"The Fortunate Painter" (1906), a story that deals primarily with the commercial side of art, introduces a theme often found in Maugham's fiction, that of the artist who lacks talent. In Paris Charles Bartle, an impoverished painter, meets Mr. Leir, a retired art dealer who made his fortune selling impressionist paintings. Leir admires Bartle's copy of a Watteau and accepts it, along with original paintings, on consignment. Through an elaborate ruse he causes customs agents in New York to conclude that he is attempting to smuggle a genuine Watteau through customs as a copy. They levy the tax due on an original, and afterward he is able to sell the copy to an American collector for a large sum. Leir pays Bartle more than he ever expected to receive for his original paintings and then destroys them.

"A Marriage of Convenience" (1908) again portrays the narrator-persona as a traveler. Taking a cargo boat from Spain, the narrator, identified as a novelist, goes ashore on an island off Tunis. Although at first he is imprisoned as a suspected spy, the sergeant, whose wife has read his novels, subsequently takes him to the French consul. The consul, Lucien Pinochet, recounts the story of his marriage to Sophie. Required by virtue of his position to be married, he places an advertisement for a wife in *Figaro* and is overwhelmed with 748 responses. In desperation he writes to Sophie, the cousin of a professor who has recommended her to him. At his first meeting he asks her hand and demands an immediate answer; she accepts, and the marriage proves happy for both. Maugham later revised the story for *The Gentleman in the Parlour*.

Although one early title, "The Mother" (1909), was included in the complete short stories with little revision, the early stories establish that Maugham was a made, not a born, writer. In his brief prefatory note to *Orientations*, written in French,[14] he described its stories as a series of attempts in varied styles and genres to discover his literary self. Through perseverance, persistence, and application to his chosen craft, he developed his talent until it brought him success. He deliberately set himself varied tasks, in part to discover where his talent lay but also because he firmly believed that a writer who makes a contribution to the literature of a nation must impose on his talent a wide range of aesthetic efforts. In his essay on Kipling, Maugham includes a passage that applies more to his own career than to Kipling's:

> As a rough generalization I would suggest that an author reaches the
> height of his powers when he is between thirty-five and forty. It takes
> him till then to learn what Kipling made a point of calling his trade.
> Till then his work is immature, tentative and experimental. By prof-
> iting by past mistakes, by the mere process of living, . . . by discov-
> ering his own limitations and learning what subjects he is competent
> to deal with and how best to deal with them, he acquires command
> over his medium. He is in possession of such talent as he has. He will
> produce the best work he is capable of for fifteen years, for twenty if
> he is lucky, and then his powers gradually dwindle.[15]

Before he wrote a story of the first rank, Maugham was in his mid-forties.

To a remarkable degree Maugham's early efforts at fiction foreshadow the prominent features of his later efforts. The similarities are such that readers familiar with Maugham's canon would have no trouble with attribution. The narrative techniques are retained, though the narrator-persona assumes an increasing importance in later stories. The settings, already highly varied, become even more exotic. The plots, readily condensed into an anecdote, foreshadow the normal plots of later fiction. Though the style, relying on colloquial dialogue and fluent idiomatic English, becomes more polished in the later writings, it is unmistakably Maugham's.

When he offered his own condemnation of the early stories, Maugham centered on their tone and their persona. He was bitter, he says, and caustic irony and satire are apparent in stories like "A Sad Case" and "Daisy." For the most part editors wanted themes that pleased the audience with gentle satire and happy conclusions. Maugham admits he could not write this kind of story, but he apparently made an effort to center his later fiction more on characters and less on society and its problems. As for the narrator, he grows more experienced and worldly, more guarded and reticent, and less judgmental as his role becomes more prominent.

Even so, the most notable legacy of Maugham's early stories is their characters. Maugham's fiction includes few children as characters and few adolescents, *Of Human Bondage* being the major exception. Over-whelmingly, his fictional characters, even in the early writings, are young or middle-aged adults. Assuming an adult and cosmopolitan audience, Maugham creates individuals whose characters have already been formed, and, like the comedy-of-manners writer, he is intent on probing beneath the surface to reveal the often incongruous elements within.

Essentially an observer of the human comedy, he does not attempt to clarify how characters became the way they are or to explore how they are altered by experience. Never one to seek out the great or famous as sources for short stories, he centers on a revelation of something unsuspected within the pattern of a seemingly ordinary life. The later exotic stories are designed to reveal the changes wrought by an alien setting, not to show how those changes occurred.

The South Sea Stories

Maugham achieved fame as a short fiction writer with 18 stories of the Southwest Pacific and Southeast Asia, published in three volumes of 6 stories each: *The Trembling of a Leaf* (1921), *The Casuarina Tree* (1926), and *Ah King* (1933). The narratives, ranging from 12,000 to 20,000 words, are lengthy by short story standards. These 18 stories were not the only fruits of Maugham's five journeys to the South Pacific and Asia between 1916 and 1926. Among other well-known works with a South Sea or Asian setting are the novels *The Moon and Sixpence* (1919), largely set in Tahiti; *The Painted Veil* (1925), set in China; and *The Narrow Corner* (1932), set in the Malay Archipelago. The travel book *On a Chinese Screen* (1922) consists of notes and sketches from Maugham's 1920 trip to China; it includes 2 stories with Chinese settings, "The Taipan" and "The Consul," that later appeared in the collected edition. *The Gentleman in the Parlour* (1930), a travel book set in Indochina, contains 4 stories later reprinted with the collected short fiction: "Masterson," "Mabel," "The Escape," and the fable "The Princess and the Nightingale." In addition, Maugham used the exotic setting for several stories published later in his career. Of these only "The Buried Talent" (1934), a story with art as a major theme, was omitted from the collected edition.

The settings for the original 18 stories are principally American Samoa and Tahiti and the Federated Malay States (modern Indonesia), including Borneo, the Malay Peninsula, and islands in the vicinity. In these areas nature produces life in lush profusion, human beings age quickly, and nature, if unchecked, quickly obliterates all human constructions. Accompanied by his helpful American secretary-companion, Gerald Haxton, Maugham amassed anecdotes, news reports, and tales for later use in his narrative art. In some stories, as Wilmon Menard discovered, [16] Maugham used actual names of characters he drew on, assuming that the remoteness of the area precluded any suits for defamation. Normally he retained the original names of islands and cities, though occasionally he invented place-names for obscure locations.

Maugham designates these *exotic* stories, a term that implies more than setting, though a remote locale is a requisite. The term is applicable as well to narratives by Conrad and Kipling, Maugham's predecessors in the genre. Exotic stories depict European and American colonials placed in an alien world that molds their characters in richly diverse ways. For some a sense of exhilaration accompanied newly discovered legal and ethical freedoms. The slow pace and easygoing life-style of the archipelagoes along the equator and the loneliness of the new inhabitants profoundly affected people accustomed to refined social conventions and keen competition with peers. While the settings offered picturesque scenery, lush tropical foliage, a placid sea, and seductive native women, the settlers also had to contend with boredom, tropical diseases and parasites, and the enervating heat of the equatorial region.

Some of Maugham's exotic characters, like Edward Barnard, find the life preferable to anything in their past. Others cling tenaciously to their more cultured and complex past and place themselves on a demanding schedule to retain their former values. Some give free rein to their latent vices and weaknesses. Bored, isolated, and lonely, they turn to drink, extramarital affairs, and crime. In all but a few, there is intellectual atrophy, for Maugham finds nothing conducive to intellectual endeavors in the region. He observes that in the colonies many men of 50 are still boys; they have ceased to develop intellectually and have continued to view life as they did in the sixth form. Though only 4 of the 18 stories derive their titles from their protagonists, their emphasis is on character. To the degree Maugham concerns himself with the role of environment in shaping character, he is reflecting his earlier naturalism.

The Trembling of a Leaf

The six stories collected in *The Trembling of a Leaf* include some of Maugham's most vivid and powerful writing. Four of the six concern failed romantic love, a common theme of his fiction. In a comprehensive study of character and theme in Maugham's stories, Abe Judson has shown that nearly two-thirds have failed love relationships as an important theme.[17] Like others of the South Sea stories, the tales cover a considerable span of time, sometimes years, for themes like the death of love require room for time to do its work.

The first story, "Mackintosh," develops the theme of male personalities in conflict. Mackintosh, an abstemious young Scotsman, is posted to a remote island as assistant to the resident, Walker, who oversees the island's copra trade. The only European there before Mackintosh arrives, he has ruled the Kanaka natives with an iron will for more than a generation, struggling to impose his work ethic on them. His principal endeavor is to build roads in order to improve the island's trading facilities. Mackintosh finds his corpulence, uncouth behavior, and imperiousness almost impossible to bear. Unlike Walker, he has not had time to modify the European elements of his own character.

But beneath Walker's crude exterior lie noble sentiments Mackintosh is slow to discern. His character reveals an undercurrent of sentimentalism that recurs in Maugham's fiction like a minor motif. Walker understands the Kanakas and looks on them as his children. Almost at retirement age, he has saved nothing for himself but has energetically promoted projects for their benefit, overriding their instinctive opposition to progress. When the natives go on strike to prevent completion of a road, he turns the tables on them with brilliant cunning. But a vindictive Kanaka, with the connivance of Mackintosh, manages to steal a pistol. Although Mackintosh warns him of the danger, Walker remains heedless of any personal peril and is mortally wounded one night.

The climax occurs at Walker's death, when he reveals his deeper nature to his subordinate. Brought back in the care of Mackintosh, he survives long enough to give instructions that no one should be punished for his murder. He urges the assistant, whom he has recommended as his replacement, to complete the road for the benefit of the natives. After Walker's death Mackintosh, crushed by guilt over misreading his superior and over his responsibility for the man's death, walks into a lagoon up to his armpits and puts a bullet through his head.

In "Red," the story Maugham later selected as his best, a crusty sea captain, somewhat resembling Walker, docks his schooner at a remote island between Apia and Pago Pago and visits Nielson, a bookish Swede with his own library who has lived there 24 years with his native mistress. Nielson narrates to him the story of Red, a young Apollo-like sailor who lived on the island many years earlier with Sally, a beautiful native girl, as his mistress. Deeply in love, they enjoyed an idyllic happiness until one day Red paddled out to trade with a whaling vessel anchored offshore and was pressed into service as a crewman, never to return. Nielson later settled on the island and fell in love with Sally. Though she finally accepted his advances and became his mistress, his sense that she held something back, that she always hoped for Red's return, denied him the bliss of requited love. Gradually his passion vanished, though he and Sally remained friends and companions. Only after the tale is completed does the captain identify himself as Red, no longer Apollo-like but now corpulent and crude. The story's ironic climax occurs when an obese old woman enters and inquires about dinner. Red has encountered Sally once again, and neither shows a trace of recognition. The story dramatically develops Maugham's most pervasive theme concerning romantic love: that "the tragedy of love is indifference."[18]

"Honolulu," the final story in the volume, explores the failure of love with an equally ironic but less poignant twist at the end. The least often reprinted story in the collection, it introduces another seaman, Captain Butler, a self-assured, self-indulgent man who pilots a modest schooner trading among the Hawaiian Islands. Butler narrates the story of his earlier experience, though Maugham's first-person narrator tells the reader he is putting the account into his own words. Butler's Kanaka mistress lives on the ship with its crew of two Kanakas and a Chinese cook. Bananas, a crewman, becomes enamored of the mistress, a development that Butler at first finds highly amusing. Later, however, he strikes Bananas for attempting to break into her cabin. Afterward the captain develops a mysterious illness, and the young woman discovers Bananas has placed a curse on him that will bring about his death before the moon enters a new phase. Countering magic with magic, she concocts a scheme that kills Bananas before his spell can kill her master. The naive narrator skeptically remarks that Butler's mistress seems too young to formulate and carry off so elaborate a scheme. His friend Winter tells him it was a different mistress: the one who saved Butler's life had later run off with the Chinese cook.

In two stories Maugham relies on changes of setting to develop his plot over time. This method eliminates the need for a character who narrates a story set in the past. In "The Pool" Lawson, a young Scotsman living in Apia, discovers Ethel, the half-caste daughter of a bankrupt merchant, Brevold, and his fourth wife, at a secluded, isolated jungle pool where she regularly goes to bathe. The incident is analogous to one in Maupassant's story "Marocca," but Maugham endows the pool with greater symbolic and psychological significance. Lawson's admiration of Ethel's beauty quickly progresses to love, and despite advice from his friends against it, he resolves to marry her. When their son is born, he decides to move back to Scotland in order to give the child better educational opportunities and a chance for a successful career. There Ethel cannot adjust to the loneliness, cold climate, and separation from her large, gregarious family. She finds a frigid mountain pool where she goes to bathe, but even this does not preserve enough of her former life to sustain her spirit. When she gets the chance, she books passage back to Samoa with her child. Lawson quits his job and follows her, but, unable to find suitable work, lapses into alcoholism. Forced to live in Brevold's noisy and crowded household, Lawson discovers that Ethel is having an affair. Despair impels him to drown himself in the pool where they first met.

In "The Fall of Edward Barnard," Maugham appears to write an ironic and lighthearted sequel to Henry James's novel *The Ambassadors*, complete with Jamesian names for the American characters. The wayward American, though, is a suitor, not a son, as in the James novel. Isabel Longstaffe, a wealthy, attractive Chicago socialite, is engaged to Edward Barnard, but before the wedding can take place, Barnard's father loses his fortune and commits suicide. To recoup his fortune Edward goes to Tahiti, where he plans to work for two years before returning to marry Isabel. After his return is delayed without explanation, a mutual friend, Bateman Hunter, who has long cherished an unspoken love for Isabel, goes to investigate.

Hunter discovers that, far from recouping his fortune, Barnard has been fired from his job and has become a friend of Arnold Jackson, Isabel's disreputable uncle, who settled in Tahiti after a financial scandal prompted him to flee Chicago. In a masochistic gesture of self-sacrifice, Bateman offers Edward a job in his own company if he will return to Chicago and marry Isabel. But Edward has found the scenery of Tahiti enchanting, and if Isabel will release him, he intends to marry Eva, Jackson's beautiful half-caste daughter. Jackson has promised to give them an island where they can have an idyllic life together. Edward has redefined success as life in a tropical paradise; Arnold can view it only as a failure. When he later reports the account to Isabel, she comments that Edward is "nobody's enemy but his own" and accepts Arnold's proposal.

"Rain," the best-known work in the collection, was Maugham's first story after a break of more than a decade. Written in 1919, it illustrates his typically linear plot line but makes significant use of symbols. Departing from the theme of failed love, it deals with the destructive force of passion in rigidly idealistic characters. The story, narrated in third person, introduces two couples who meet on board a liner, Dr. and Mrs. Macphail, traveling to his new practice in Apia, and the Reverend Mr. Davidson and his wife, returning to their posts as medical missionaries to islands north of Samoa after a one-year leave. They keep company on the ship because neither couple likes the heavy drinking and card playing that go on in the lounge. When their ship is quarantined at Pago Pago, they find themselves housed in a crowded, dilapidated rooming house during the rainy season, and their acquaintance grows closer.

There they meet Sadie Thompson, another passenger, whom Mr. Davidson soon identifies as a fugitive from Iwelei, the red-light district of Honolulu. When she begins entertaining sailors with raucous parties in her room, Davidson attempts personal intervention to restore propriety, only to be manhandled by Sadie's guests. He then influences Horn, the owner, to forbid the parties and persuades the American governor to deport Sadie on the next boat back to San Francisco, where prison awaits her. Her pleas to be permitted to go to Australia instead fall on deaf ears.

Not content simply to ensure her just punishment, Davidson resolves to save her soul, and Sadie, now desperate, is receptive to prayer in her room. After a few sessions Davidson assures Macphail that she is a changed person. On her final evening in Samoa, when all stands in readiness for her departure to San Francisco, Davidson holds a late-night prayer session with Sadie. The following morning an excited Horn summons Macphail to the beach to examine Davidson's body, dead from a self-inflicted wound. After Mrs. Davidson is told of the death, they hear Sadie's phonograph blaring its raucous music. As she exclaims at the top of her voice that all men are pigs, Dr. Macphail gasps, "He understood" (*Complete Stories*, vol. 1, 39).

No story better illustrates Maugham's gift at character revelation through brief descriptions. The severe, narrow fanaticism of the Davidsons, in sharp contrast to the worldly tolerance of Dr. Macphail, is evident in the description of Mrs. Davidson:

> She was dressed in black and wore round her neck a gold chain from which dangled a small cross. She was a little woman, with brown, dull hair very elaborately arranged, and she had prominent blue eyes behind her invisible *pince-nez*. Her face was long, like a sheep's, but she gave no impression of foolishness, rather of extreme alertness; she had the quick movements of a bird. The most remarkable thing about her was her voice, high, metallic, and without inflection; it fell on the ear with a hard monotony, irritating to the nerves like the pitiless clamour of the pneumatic drill. (*Complete Stories*, vol. 1, 2)

Maugham's use of visual, sound, and kinetic imagery creates the impression of a rigid character, one forever set on its course. When Mrs. Davidson explains to the bemused Dr. Macphail how her husband had created a sense of sin in the natives and how as missionaries they were able to bring anyone who defied them into submission, the picture of ruthless fanaticism becomes clear. The description of Mr. Davidson, on the other hand, suggests an internal struggle to keep himself on the arduous course he has chosen:

> His appearance was singular. He was very tall and thin, with long limbs loosely jointed; hollow cheeks and curiously high cheek-bones; He had so cadaverous an air that it surprised you to notice how thin and sensual were his lips. He wore his hair very long. His dark eyes, set deep in their sockets, were large and tragic; and his hands, with their big, long fingers, were finely shaped; they gave him a look of great strength. But the most striking thing about him was the feeling he gave you of suppressed fire. It was impressive and vaguely troubling. He was not a man with whom any intimacy was possible. (*Complete Stories*, vol. 1, 6)

The uneasy combination of qualities described in Davidson serves to foreshadow his fate. The setting itself, no longer alluring like that of "The Fall of Edward Barnard," becomes symbolic of the tragedy, for the incessant tropical rain beating against the metal roof of the rooming house grates on the occupants' nerves, and the clouds cast a gray pall over the luxuriant nature outside. Further symbolism occurs when Davidson reveals that he has been dreaming about the mountains of Nebraska, and Dr. Macphail recalls that the mountains are shaped like female breasts.

The Casuarina Tree

The stories included in *The Casuarina Tree* are set in the Federated Malay States, hundreds of miles west of Tahiti and Samoa, settings for *The Trembling of a Leaf*. In his preface Maugham explains that the casuarina tree, which grows along the shores of tropical lands as if to protect the land from storms, suggests "the planters and administrators who . . . have after all brought to the peoples among whom they dwell tranquillity, justice, and welfare."[19] The volume introduces as characters British colonials carrying out their administrative duties in a remote portion of the empire. Maugham makes it clear, however, that the colonials he depicted were the exceptional ones, not the average colonial officials he met. Of the six stories four deal with failed human relationships, involving broken marriages, love triangles, and adultery. Two, like "Mackintosh," concern poorly matched men serving together at an isolated outpost.

"The Outstation," among Maugham's most compelling stories, contrasts two male types, Mr. Warburton, the resident at a remote outpost, and Allen Cooper, his young assistant who arrives just as the story opens. Warburton is one of Maugham's most memorable and fantastic characters, and the narrative lavishes detail on him. A consummate snob, he had gained access to the English upper class through his inherited fortune and lived a life of partying, good company, and exclusive clubs. Aware that his hold on society was tenuous at best, he reacted with a combination of bravado and nonchalance, and eventually his passion for gambling cost him his fortune. With no inherited income and no preparation for life in a profession or business, the middle-aged Warburton left everything that mattered behind and went to the colonies to earn a living.

But in Malaya he maintains, insofar as possible, his former life-style. Every morning at breakfast he reads an issue of the *London Times*, exactly six weeks old, to maintain ties and to preserve the cherished illusion that he remains a part of society. He continues a correspondence with great ladies in England whom he knew and regularly sends notes of congratulation or condolence as the situations require. Every evening he dresses formally for dinner, even though he habitually dines alone. A capable administrator, he runs his station with admirable efficiency, though his superiors find his snobbery a source of amusement.

Nonetheless, like Walker in "Mackintosh," he develops a paternalistic attitude toward the native Malays and even a sentimental attachment to them. He understands their character and admires their virtues, while at the same time ignoring their vices. He instinctively knows how far he can push them, and he carefully observes the limits. Since his methods have gained him their trust and loyalty, he can carry on his operation with a mixture of gentleness and firmness. Never does he permit himself to become so familiar with them as to take a native mistress: "A man who had been called George by Albert Edward, Prince of Wales, could hardly be expected to have any connection with a native" (*Complete Stories*, vol. 1, 276). No one could have suspected that his will provided for his remains to be buried among the natives he had grown to love.

Cooper, by contrast, is an inexperienced youth with a common background and a poor education who nurses grievances of his own. Though a good worker, he creates difficulties for himself through his harsh, peremptory treatment of the Malays and shows an equal lack of tact when dealing with the resident. At his first dinner with Warburton, he arrives unkempt, poorly dressed, and dirty, to find Warburton dressed in formal dinner attire. Although Warburton's initial impression of Cooper is unfavorable, he invites him to dinner a second time. There matters go better until Cooper, having consumed too much wine, brings up Warburton's snobbery and the relationship is forever damaged. The final break occurs months later, after Warburton leaves the post under Cooper's charge while he travels. On his return he discovers that Cooper has disarranged his bundle of newspapers while looking through them for details of a murder case. After a bitter confrontation, though they continue to live in close proximity, they meet only for official matters.

Once, after Cooper has broken the rules regarding the work hours for natives, Warburton has to reprimand him. But Cooper is unwilling to accept his chief's guidance. His servants resent his tyrannical treatment and abandon him. He withholds wages from his houseboy Abbas and in anger strikes him down on one occasion, heedless of the vengeful streak in the Malay character. Warburton, who knows everything that happens at his post, feels it necessary to warn Cooper of the danger he has brought on himself, but the headstrong subordinate is heedless. Warburton's subsequent attempt to transfer him is rejected by the sultan's English secretary, who assumes Warburton makes too much of his assistant's humble origins. Yet as Warburton recognizes, once Cooper has battered Abbas, his fate is sealed. Summoned by the servants early one morning, Warburton finds Cooper lying dead in his bungalow with a kris in his back. Abbas will be punished by brief imprisonment and afterward made a servant in Warburton's house.

Essentially a story of character conflict, "The Outstation" offers more extensive character portrayal than the usual Maugham narrative. Ironically, Warburton, the snob, represents the capable, just, and enlightened administrator, whereas Cooper, whose origins should have prepared him for the role, fails utterly. As with several other Maugham stories, the major conflict, while centering on the two main characters, does not lead to the tragic conclusion.

In "The Yellow Streak" one encounters another character who strives to maintain a mask of respectability. Izzart, a Eurasian educated at an English public school, attempts to conceal his mother's true identity by saying she was Spanish, for he knows the English believe that all Eurasians have a yellow streak and cannot be trusted when the chips are down. He is assigned as a guide to Campion, an engineer exploring commercial mining possibilities in Malaya. During a river journey their dugout is swamped by a tidal wave, and Izzart leaves Campion to fend for himself in the rushing, turbulent water. When he discovers to his surprise that Campion has survived, he fears the others will accuse him of cowardice. In his report to the chief at Kuala Solor, he claims that Campion was drunk but learns from the official in charge, again to his surprise, that Campion has reported before him. Exasperated, he later admits his cowardice to Campion, only to learn that Campion in no way holds him responsible. Ironically, he asks only that Izzart not reflect badly on him when he reports, for he knows Izzart has a yellow streak. Although the Maugham persona does not appear in the story, the writer draws on his own experience for the central episode. Traveling with his secretary Gerald Haxton and native guides up a Borneo river, Maugham almost drowned when a wave overturned their dugout. The experience, however, revealed no cowardice, for Maugham's companion bravely helped to save him.

If "The Outstation" represents the Maugham story most often found in anthologies, "The Letter" is probably more widely known through its stage and screen versions. One of many narratives with adultery as a theme, it was the only story Maugham himself rewrote for the stage, where it enjoyed a phenomenal success. Three movie versions, the most recent starring Lee Remick, brought it to an immense audience. Based on an actual murder trial that occurred in Malaya some 20 years before Maugham's journey there, the story is highly dramatic. It illustrates Maugham's common theme that punishment does not always follow a crime.

Gerald Hammond has a reputation as a ladies' man, and the older men at the club predict that one day it will get him into trouble. No one is greatly surprised when he is shot by Leslie Crosbie, who explains that he appeared at her house at night while her husband was away and attempted to rape her. Although everyone is certain Leslie will be acquitted, formality requires that she face trial, and to the dismay of her husband, Robert, she awaits her trial in jail. Preparing her defense, her shrewd lawyer, Mr. Joyce, points out to her a possible problem the prosecution might seize on: Leslie shot Hammond six times, firing several times after he had fallen to the ground. She explains, quite plausibly, that she was naturally distraught and did not fully realize what she was doing.

But before the trial a further complication unexpectedly arises. From his astute, ambitious Chinese clerk, Mr. Joyce learns that Hammond's Chinese mistress has a letter from Leslie to Hammond. A handwritten copy convinces Joyce that the letter—in which Leslie invites Hammond to come to her house on the evening of his death—might be damaging were it to fall into the hands of the prosecution, and he arranges for Robert to buy it for £10,000. At the trial Leslie is easily acquitted, but afterward Robert returns to their estate alone, leaving her with the Joyces while he decides what to do. Both Robert and Mr. Joyce realize Leslie killed Hammond because of jealousy. The story qualifies as a murder mystery, and although the mystery is solved, the guilty person goes unpunished. It features a galaxy of interesting characters and exceptionally strong dramatic conflict.

In "P&O" an embittered Mrs. Hamelyn, having divorced her husband of 20 years for a recent affair, returns to England aboard a P&O liner. On board she meets an Irish planter, Gallagher, returning for retirement after abandoning his native mistress, who has sworn he will not reach land alive. Inexplicably, he develops hiccups that cannot be stopped. Following his death and burial at sea on Christmas Day, Mrs. Hamelyn writes a letter of forgiveness to her former husband.

In "The Force of Circumstance," a spouse is unable to forgive, and Maugham develops a plot that includes some inherent improbabilities. Guy, a Malayan colonial official on leave in England, marries Doris and takes her with him back to Malaya. To his surprise he is sent back to his former station, where at first Doris is quite content. But then she notices a Malayan woman who lurks about the house and has to be driven off by servants; later she notices a Eurasian child in the village. Guy acknowledges the woman had been his mistress for several years before his return to England and says he had given her a cash settlement, not expecting to return to the same post. Shaken by the confession, Doris requests time to think it over, and decides to return to England. The story reflects Maugham's interest in the unpredictability of people's reactions in love relationships; typically, he refrains from exploring the motives that might account for Doris's reaction but leaves it as a reflection of her character.

"Before the Party" has an English setting by way of a frame and illustrates Maugham's technique of building a story around an anecdote. It also illustrates how a long-kept secret, once revealed, changes people's lives. Mr. and Mrs. Albert Skinner and their daughters, Millicent and Kathleen, are preparing to leave for a garden party given by Canon Hayward in honor of the bishop of Hong Kong. The ordinary details of dress and preparation of the three women create an atmosphere of bustle and social propriety, but Mrs. Skinner sets the course of the story by inquiring why the bishop had said that Harold, Millicent's late husband, committed suicide, when Millicent told them he died of a fever. In response Millicent narrates the story of her married life with Harold in Borneo.

It is the story of marriage to an alcoholic, whose addiction was only aggravated by the struggles of life in a hostile environment. After years of Harold's broken promises, pleas for forgiveness, and relapses, Millicent returned home from a trip to Kuala Solor, where she had sought medical help for their teenage daughter. She discovered Harold in a drunken stupor; unable to rouse him, she killed him with a Malay sword. When the assistant returned after Harold's death, she explained it as suicide, and no one raised any questions. Shocked by the revelation of murder, her stunned family know it must remain a secret, and they leave for the party as planned.

Within this story events that occurred over several years are narrated within the time required to prepare for a party and leave. In *Traveller's Library* Maugham wrote of Aldous Huxley, "I think it possible that a short story should occupy itself with a single moment of time. I was interested to see how Aldous Huxley . . . in a story called *Chawdron*, in which he related events that occurred over many years, used the device of making the narrator tell the story to a friend in the interval between breakfast and luncheon."[20]

Ah King

All six stories collected in *Ah King* concern the theme of marriage. The book takes its title from a faithful Chinese servant who accompanied Maugham on a six-week journey through Borneo, Indochina, and Thailand. Except for "The Vessel of Wrath," the stories, set primarily in Malaya and the Dutch East Indies, treat of failed relationships and dark secrets.

In "The Vessel of Wrath," Maugham uses a third-person narrative that requires more than a year for development. The story introduces a galaxy of lively characters inhabiting the Alas Islands, a fictional chain in the Dutch East Indies. A brother-sister missionary team, Martha and Owen Jones, minister energetically to the medical and spiritual needs of the natives. Miss Jones, a nondescript woman of 40, possesses aplomb, energy, and ability and, though reserved by nature, optimistically believes that good, while sometimes latent, exists within every human being. Her brother, inclined to look to the darker sides of human nature, feels compelled to denounce an English beachcomber and wastrel, Edmund Wilson, nicknamed Ginger Ted, for drunken brawling. As a result of the missionary's complaint, the Dutch controller, Gruyter, despite his more tolerant view of human nature, sentences Ginger Ted to six months' hard labor; because of Ted's past brushes with the law, Gruyter is unwilling to consider probation. The story develops through a series of sparkling episodes bringing Ginger Ted and Miss Jones together. Gradually she reforms him, and he announces to the astonished Gruyter that they are to be married.

"The Book Bag" and "The Back of Beyond" illustrate how an excessively emotional reaction to bad news exposes a dark secret carried by the protagonists. "The Back of Beyond" represents a skillful narrative at three levels. The plot unfolds during a meeting between George Moon, a district officer in Malaya, and Tom Saffrey, a rubber planter who seeks his advice. On the initial level, much of the characterization and description of setting occurs through the reverie of Moon, a 55-year-old official on the verge of retirement. At a second level Tom Saffrey explains how he discovered his wife's infidelity through her excessive grief over news of the death at sea of Knobby Clark, a friend and fellow planter. At a third level the plot features Saffrey reporting to Moon the story of his wife's affair as she told it. The story is placed in context at the end when Moon, recalling his divorce of his wife for a similar affair, counsels Tom to forget about it. "The right thing is the kind thing," he tells him (*Collected Stories*, vol. 1, 910).

Moon, the older and wiser man, represents one of Maugham's *raisonneurs* who view life with tolerant and kindly detachment. After Moon cautions Saffrey that he can expect no gratitude for his generosity, Saffrey labels him a cynic, a term frequently applied to Maugham. The mild-mannered district officer offers a worldly wise defense: " 'I haven't deeply considered the matter,' smiled George Moon, 'but if to look truth in the face and not resent it when it's unpalatable, and take human nature as you find it, smiling when it's absurd and grieved without exaggeration when it's pitiful, is to be cynical, then I suppose I'm a cynic. Mostly human nature is both absurd and pitiful, but if life has taught you tolerance you find in it more to smile at than to weep' " (*Collected Stories*, vol. 1, 910). A detached rational analyst like Moon, the story suggests, can minimize the damage wrought by human foibles, and Saffrey wisely accepts his advice.

"The Book Bag" represents a more artful and intricate narrative. The form is a complex application of a narrative convention Maugham frequently uses: the narrator meets a character with a story to tell, and then the story unfolds from the character's point of view, though the narrator assumes a minor role in the story. In "The Book Bag" the narrator, a successful author, is invited by Mark Featherstone, a district officer, to the local club at his post. He becomes acquainted with some of the English residents through playing bridge in a skilled, low-key manner. He talks with Featherstone about books and lends him a biography of Byron from the heavy bag of books he takes on his travels as a precaution against running out of reading material in remote places. The narrator sometimes offers his advice when he is asked and, during Featherstone's narrative, occasionally prompts him with pointed questions.

Featherstone's story concerns Olive and Tim Hardy, a brother and sister whose early loss of both parents kept them together in an effort to make a fortune as planters and thereby retain their family estate in England. Featherstone, a friend and frequent guest in their home, fell in love with Olive, but she treated his ardor with coolness. When Tim traveled to England on business, Featherstone pressed his suit and found her no more enthusiastic. After Tim wrote that he had married while in England, Olive grew distraught with grief. Following Tim's return with his bride, Olive, like Ibsen's Hedda Gabler, committed suicide by shooting herself. Despite the foreshadowing that occurs early in the story, such as the mention of Byron's incest, the cause of Olive's suicide is not evident until the story's end. Featherstone, the only Englishman in Malaya known to her, assisted Tim's wife in her return to England.

"Footprints in the Jungle," like "The Letter," is an exotic story that also qualifies as a mystery tale. Amid a calm, serene setting, it recounts a grisly murder that occurred 20 years earlier. The details are as carefully handled as they would be in a detective story. The narrator plays bridge at the club in Tanah Merah, Malaya, an original Dutch town set in a place of natural beauty. His partner, Gaze, is a police major nearing retirement. The other couple, Theo Cartwright and his wife, prove the better players. Gaze, the narrator notes, bids somewhat recklessly and counts on the defense to make mistakes in order to make the contract. The story illustrates how Gaze's bridge play reveals his fundamental character, for he has acted similarly as a police investigator. After the Cartwrights leave with their 20-year-old daughter, Olive, Gaze begins over cigars an account of these two ordinary people.

He recalls investigating the murder of Reggie Bronson, Mrs. Cartwright's first husband, near his estate in Selantan. He had been shot while traveling by bicycle over a remote jungle trail. The murder occurred in late afternoon, and by the time Gaze and the accompanying doctor reached the scene, night had fallen. Little could be found except Bronson's footprints beside the trail where he had stopped before being shot. Robbery was the apparent motive, since his billfold and watch were missing. Unable to discover any significant clues, Gaze decided to wait for evidence that some native was spending money freely and then make an arrest.

Shortly after the murder Cartwright, who had been living with the Bronsons while looking for a job, found work elsewhere and moved away. After Olive was born, Mrs. Bronson joined Cartwright and married him. Later Gaze uncovered clues that ruled out robbery as a motive and realized that Cartwright had killed Bronson. The evidence came too late, though, for him to make a case against the Cartwrights, and officially the murder remained unsolved. By chance a new assignment brought him to the place where the Cartwrights were living, and now at Tanah Merah they are often in the same social circles.

The narrator occasionally intervenes in the leisurely account to ask a question or make a remark calculated to elicit a response. Gaze has little confidence that he can tell the story well, but the narrator, a successful writer, offers reassurance and encouragement. Ironically, Gaze has the final word and turns the tables at the end, becoming Maugham's *raisonneur*. The narrator suggests that the Cartwrights must be very ill at ease in their company. No, Gaze says, people do not worry much about their crimes if they are confident they won't be caught. In response the narrator hazards the view that the Cartwrights cannot be very nice people, and Gaze counters with a litany of their virtues, assuring him that they are very nice people. They were guilty of a horrible crime, but the act did not reflect their basic character.

Both "Neil MacAdam" and "The Door of Opportunity" combine the marriage theme and the motif of art, a theme often found in the later stories. The title character of "Neil MacAdam," an innocent young Scot, arrives in Kuala Solor, Malaya, where he serves as assistant to Angus Munro, the museum curator. There he catches the eye of Munro's passionate Russian wife, Darya. Though her pursuit of MacAdam begins with a shared interest in literature, he is slow to recognize her actual intent. During an expedition to a remote site, he flees from her obvious advances into the jungle at night. Attempting to follow him, Darya becomes lost and perishes in a storm, leaving her husband inconsolable.

"The Door of Opportunity" begins in England, with Alban and Anne Torel journeying by train from Tilbury to London, where they check into a fashionable hotel. The story unfolds as a flashback in the mind of

Anne while her husband is away at his club before dinner. In Daktar, Sondurah, where Alban had been district officer, the Torels kept aloof from other colonials, regarding them as second-rate. Although Anne was certain that one day Alban would be governor, an incident in their district dashed their hopes. Chinese coolies had staged an uprising at a remote plantation, and, against Anne's advice, Alban decided to wait for reinforcements before going to suppress it. By the time he arrived with his reinforced company, a Dutch planter in the area, with assistance from two of his men, had put down the rebellion and arrested its leaders, to the embarrassment of British colonial authorities. What Alban regarded as prudent delay the governor considered cowardice, and proceeded to dismiss him.

After Alban returns from his club, Anne announces she is leaving him, reproaching him as she does: "We did think ourselves better than the rest of them because we loved literature and art and music, we weren't content to live a life of ignoble jealousies and vulgar tittle-tattle, we did cherish things of the spirit, and we loved beauty. . . . They laughed at us and sneered at us. . . . We didn't care. We called them Philistines. . . . Our justification was that we were better and nobler and wiser and braver than they were. And you weren't better, you weren't nobler, you weren't braver" (*Complete Stories*, vol. 1, 878–79). She reflects the view that Maugham emphasized in *The Summing Up*: the only justification for art is that it promotes right action.

Stories of relationships in *Ah King* develop a theme found elsewhere in Maugham: that the woman, often an older woman, initiates the relationship and determines its ending, particularly where adultery is concerned. The theme of marital infidelity so pervades Maugham's fiction that V. S. Pritchett equated Maugham's idea of the white man's burden with his wife's infidelity.[21] In "The Back of Beyond," the passion that begins the relationship seems mutual, but Violet Moon clearly makes the decision to end the affair when she discovers Enid Clark is pregnant. Miss Jones's comical pursuit of Ginger Ted in "The Vessel of Wrath" is entirely one-sided, reminiscent of Ann Whitefield's pursuit of John Tanner in Shaw's *Man and Superman*. She manages the affair with persistence and optimism and brings about a humorous and constructive conclusion, for she not only reforms and marries Ted but gives him a new purpose in life. In "The Book Bag" Olive Hardy is a year older than her brother, Tim, and when he sees a picture of the two, the narrator comments that her appearance suggests the stronger character. Her suicide and events leading up to it portray her as a person of extremely strong will. In "The Door of Opportunity," Anne Torel shows strong self-discipline by concealing her decision to leave her husband until they reach London. Even in "Footprints in the Jungle," Gaze tells the narrator that Mrs. Cartwright obviously had planned the murder and persuaded Theo to carry it out, a conclusion he reaches from her physiognomy. In "Neil MacAdam" Darya's relentless pursuit makes her responsibility for her affairs apparent, though the plot introduces an additional theme, that of the price of virtue. Yet another illicit affair could hardly have been so devastating to her husband as her death was. As Judson observes (257), rarely is an English or American protagonist of a Maugham story either aggressive or violent, though Cartwright is a significant exception. If English or American males display aggression, it is normally directed against themselves. Most murders in Maugham's fiction are committed either by foreigners or by females.

Ashenden; or, The British Agent and Six Stories Written in the First Person Singular

As its preface explains, the 16 stories in *Ashenden; or, The British Agent* were based on Maugham's experience as a British intelligence agent during World War I. A realistic depiction of the experiences of a workaday spy, the book became required reading for MI6 agents during World War II. When World War I began, Maugham volunteered for service in an ambulance unit and was posted to France, where he spent several months caring for wounded soldiers. On leave in England in summer 1915, he was introduced by his future wife, Syrie Wellcome, to Sir John Wallinger, chief of British Military Intelligence for France and Switzerland. Realizing that Maugham's knowledge of French and German might prove useful and that his status as a writer afforded a convenient cover, Wallinger recruited him for military intelligence. In fall 1915 Maugham traveled to Geneva to replace an agent who had suffered a nervous breakdown. Declining any remuneration, he undertook a variety of missions, but, if his stories and general comments are to be trusted, none were especially dramatic. He found the atmosphere of Switzerland congenial to his imagination, for, like Malaya, the neutral country attracted exotic and flamboyant individuals of varied races and nationalities. Some were there to escape the perils of war, but many, like Ashenden, were involved in espionage activities.

Concerning Maugham's actual duties, much mystery remains and no doubt will do so forever. In Switzerland he regularly crossed Lake Geneva to the French village of Thonon, bearing information. In 1916, after a year's service in Switzerland, he traveled to America and made his first South Sea journey to Samoa to gather material for fiction and possibly to carry out intelligence work as well. It is noteworthy that administrative control of Samoa was divided between the United States and Germany.

After returning to New York in 1917, Maugham was posted to Russia by Sir William Wiseman, head of British intelligence in America. He was given access to large sums of money in the interest of supporting the

Kerensky government, so as to prevent the Bolsheviks from seizing power and Russia from withdrawing from the war. He acknowledged candidly that his mission was a failure, but in one context pointedly suggests that, given more time, he might have succeeded. In the fictional version the settings for Ashenden's espionage activities are limited to France, Switzerland, Italy, and Russia. After his return from Russia, Maugham entered a Scottish sanatorium for treatment of tuberculosis; this experience became the basis of a later Ashenden story, "Sanatorium."

The name Ashenden, like numerous others in Maugham's fiction, is common in Kent, where he spent his boyhood. It was in fact the surname of a schoolmate at the King's School, Canterbury. The points of identity between Maugham and his alter ego, who serves to unify narratives that are primarily about others, are too numerous to list. He is fluent in German and French, has studied a year at Heidelberg, and has produced novels, short stories, and plays. He recalls having seen Ibsen drinking German beer in a Heidelberg café. He has a pale complexion, and, like his creator, Ashenden enjoys spending his leisure time either reading or playing bridge or patience.

Ashenden is a cultured and cosmopolitan writer who approaches intelligence work with detachment, a sense of irony, and a talent for careful observation of human beings. He works unobtrusively and efficiently, according to a regular schedule. Ostensibly writing a play, he leaves the manuscript easily in sight of visitors to his room yet carefully avoids putting in writing anything that might suggest his true purpose. He is pleased to be known as a successful novelist and playwright and is flattered when a customs agent who has read his short stories lets his baggage pass uninspected. Although he finds intelligence work inherently dull, he is not bored by his fellow human beings, for they are his "raw material." Like his chief, R, he prefers knaves to fools. He reveals a touch of snobbery when he gives R his fashionable London address as 36 Chesterfield Street, Mayfair (Maugham's was 6 Cadogan Street, Mayfair). While he is basically tolerant, he contemplates the deaths of traitors and enemy agents with indifference, and it never occurs to him to be disloyal to his nation or class. Though he often views his fellow human beings with interest and sympathy, he is given to flippancy and ironic asides in response to dullness or clumsy attempts at humor.

Unlike the Maugham persona of earlier stories, Ashenden occasionally assumes an important role in the narratives. He forces other people into courses of action necessary to his work or manipulates them in ways he is told to. He receives his instructions from R, realizing that his assignment is only a minor piece in a larger puzzle. At times the purposes of his actions are concealed even from him. He writes lengthy reports and, growing to believe no one reads them, injects humor into one, as Maugham had done, the result of this levity being a reprimand from superiors. Despite his extensive presence, Ashenden serves primarily not as a man of action but an interviewer, courier, informant, or escort.

The only other character who reappears regularly is Ashenden's chief, identified only by his initial, "R," though several characters recur in two or three stories. Even R is sometimes limited to a flashback in Ashenden's mind or makes his presence felt only through written messages. Further unifying elements are Maugham's recurrent themes and his tendency to introduce, at the conclusion of one story, a character or theme to be developed in the subsequent episode. Narrative strands like these made it simpler for Maugham later to combine two or more stories under a single title for the collected edition.

"R," the first story, is exceptionally brief. Ashenden is summoned to a house where he is to meet his chief, an intelligence officer, the only other character in the story. Ashenden sizes up his superior as cunning, ruthless, and intelligent, carefully noting his cold blue eyes set too close together, so that they seem to stare through others. Uneasy with strangers and socially insecure, R jocularly talks about Ashenden's profession and suggests intelligence work might offer him rich material. He gives as an example an account of a recent occurrence, outlining a plot involving theft of papers by a woman who meets an agent in a bar, takes him to her room, and drugs him into a sound sleep; on awakening, the agent discovers that the woman and his file of secret documents are missing. Ashenden replies that writers have been using that plot for years and reality has only just caught up with them. As the two part, R gives Ashenden some advice that Ashenden accepts as sound: "If you do well you'll get no thanks and if you get into trouble you'll get no help" (*Complete Stories*, vol. 1, 439).

As a spy story that illuminates the nature of Ashenden's work in Switzerland, "Gustav" represents a succinct example. Gustav Grabow, a Swiss businessman who often has occasion to cross the German border, is hired as an intelligence source for the British. R at first praises his detailed and fulsome reports but later grows suspicious about Gustav and sends Ashenden to Basel to investigate. Ashenden discovers that instead of securing information from journeys across the enemy border, Gustav has been compiling his reports from German newspapers and from travelers who cross into Switzerland. Once he ascertains that Gustav has not been working simultaneously for the Germans, Ashenden is amused by his ingenuity and deception. Before Ashenden departs, Gustav provides useful information about an English turncoat living in Switzerland, the subject of another story.

The story illustrates the mundane, routine nature of Ashenden's normal activities, totally lacking in glamour. When on one occasion he slips a pistol into his coat, he considers his precaution melodramatic. Some of his missions end in failure, some take surprising turns, and some conclude as planned. The reader encounters the usual devices of spy fiction—coded messages, false passports, aliases, disguises, clandestine meetings, intrigue, sudden journeys, and, permeating the work, an atmosphere of mystery created by the need to conceal information and identities. But far from bearing an aura of mystery, these elements are made to appear commonplace and even a bit tawdry. One finds in the espionage stories that Maugham's realism, manifested in careful attention to detail and to motivation of characters, enlivens the narrative. In *The Summing Up* he explains that audiences are strictly deterministic, unwilling to accept unmotivated or inadequately motivated actions. Maugham's characters arouse interest in part because they are striking and unusual, but he takes care to clarify their motives.

Like the earlier Maugham persona, Ashenden elicits personal stories from his interlocutors, an indication that he inspires their confidence. In "Miss King" the title character, an English governess for an Egyptian family, is dying and summons Ashenden. Despite his comforting, reassuring bedside manner, she dies without revealing anything, having exclaimed only the word *England* at her death. On the other hand, the British ambassador in "His Excellency" narrates a poignant story of an early love affair and bares his soul to a point Ashenden finds embarrassing. Of the 16 stories in the volume, this one most resembles the South Sea stories. Ashenden dines with someone who has a story to tell and after dinner hears a tale that strips off a mask, so that he can view the character behind it. He had not suspected that beneath Sir Herbert's prim formality and behind his dazzlingly successful career lay a soul embittered by the loss of early love. Like "Miss King," the story has nothing to do with an espionage mission.

"The Traitor," by contrast, illustrates the ambiguities surrounding Ashenden's role as an agent. Under the alias "Mr. Somerville"—a name actually used by Maugham—Ashenden meets the English exile Grantly Caypor and his German wife at a Swiss inn where they are living. R has instructed Ashenden to become acquainted with Caypor, a botanist known to be a German agent, and has hinted that Caypor might be useful as a recruit. While Caypor poses little danger in Switzerland, he has exposed one of R's agents to the Germans, with the result that the man was arrested and shot. R is unwilling to forget this event and expects Caypor to pay a price.

Ashenden tells the Caypors that he is on leave from the Censorship Department while recovering from an illness, and persuades Caypor's wife to tutor him in German. As for recruiting Caypor, Ashenden quickly concludes that the man is too unreliable; he has no way of knowing that Caypor's German contact is pressing Caypor to provide more information and suggesting that a job in England might prove useful. When Caypor asks Ashenden about a job in the Censorship Department, on the pretext that he can no longer avoid doing his part for England, Ashenden provides him with a visa and a letter of recommendation, for he has grasped the insidious purpose of R's vague instructions: once Caypor crosses the border into France, R will have him arrested and shot. Although Ashenden had understood the overall problem as R explained it, R could give only vague orders about what he should do. As the story develops, the plan formulates itself, and R's objective is attained.

When he conflated the 16 Ashenden stories into 6 for the collected edition, Maugham omitted "The Flip of a Coin," a short tale with an ambiguous conclusion. In a brief narrative Ashenden discusses a plan to blow up German munitions factories in Austria with Herbartus, a Polish saboteur. Herbartus points out that the action would cause the death and dismemberment of hundreds of his fellow citizens, forced to work in the factories. As he contemplates seeking his chief's approval, Ashenden recalls in a mental flashback an earlier episode with R. An assassin had proposed to kill King B., ruler of a neutral Balkan country, who was sympathetic toward Germany, and since the assassin asked for £5,000, Ashenden had to consult R. Initially R responded with indignation: "We don't wage war by those methods. We leave them to the Germans. Damn it all, we are gentlemen."[22] When he asked why Ashenden didn't knock the man down, Ashenden sheepishly replied that the man was larger. But after a pause R resumed the subject in a different tone. It would, of course, be quite a good thing to have the king out of the way, and if anyone, motivated by patriotic duty, chose to assume that responsibility, then R could not seriously object. Ashenden made it plain that he would not sponsor the assassination with his own money. Returning to the question at hand, he reflects on the consequences of the proposed sabotage. He suggests they decide the issue by flipping a coin. As he uncovers it after the toss, he observes, "Well, that's that."

The conclusion that leaves the reader uncertain represents a traditional narrative device drawn from stories like Frank Stockton's "The Lady or the Tiger." That this device violates Maugham's sense of form may account for his omission of a well-written tale. In *A Writer's Notebook* he expressed his view of a story's conclusion: "I want a story to have form, and I don't see how you can give it that unless you can bring it to a conclusion that leaves no legitimate room for questioning. But even if you could bring yourself to leave your reader up in the air you don't want to leave yourself up in the air with him" (*Notebook*, 268).

A story with a more typical Maugham ending, "Love and Russian Literature," introduces the unique phenomenon of the less-than-ardent Maugham persona in love. The story develops after Ashenden meets Czech operatives in Petrograd who are to help him carry out his mission. He asks them for information about his former mistress Anastasia Alexandrovna, whose character is a thinly disguised portrayal of Sasha Kropotkin, a Russian exile with whom Maugham had an affair prior to World War I. As if seeking to create further distance from the subject, Maugham has Ashenden recall his affair with Anastasia in a flashback. Their relationship developed in London during a period of enthusiasm for Russian culture—its literature, music, and ballet—abetted by a colony of Russian revolutionary exiles. Ashenden, caught up in the enthusiasm, had come to know several of the Russians living near him. After he met Anastasia, the two were often in each other's company at social gatherings. When he declared his affection for her, she assured him their feelings were mutual. He then brought up the matter of her husband, Vladimir Seminovich Leonidov, a drab person whom Ashenden believed thoroughly unworthy of her. Pointing out the complexity of divorce in England, he suggested they weigh the difficulties before matters progressed too far. In response Anastasia assured him that Vladimir would never put her through the humiliation of a divorce action; once she announced her desire to marry Ashenden, he would simply remove any obstacle by committing suicide.

Ashenden, somewhat taken aback, suggests that if a life is at stake, they had better be certain their love is worth it, and Anastasia offers a solution. They will travel to Paris and spend a week together to test their love. As they proceed to have a culturally rich week, visiting museums and attending concerts, they discover one problem. Anastasia orders scrambled eggs every morning for breakfast. Ashenden accepts this for two mornings but on the third asks for fried eggs. The emotional Anastasia takes him to task for creating difficulties for the cook, an act that shows him insensitive to the struggles of the proletariat. Reluctantly, Ashenden resigns himself to eating scrambled eggs every morning. On their return to London, he books the first available Cunard liner for New York, thus ending the affair by fleeing. When he later meets Anastasia in Petrograd, she tells him Vladimir has left her for a member of the intelligentsia, a writer on political economy, and they are to have a baby. Ashenden realizes that what he loved in her was not herself but the reflection of Russian culture and literature he perceived in her.

Through his work Ashenden becomes acquainted with a host of memorable and outlandish characters, some of them drawn from actual people Maugham met. The exotic dancer Guilia Lazzari submits to his will and lures her lover, the Indian agitator Chandra Lal, to captivity and death. Her tormented passion for Lal is undercut by her calculating self-interest when she learns of his death. She asks Ashenden to obtain for her the expensive watch she had given Lal, which he was wearing at the time. The most flamboyant character, Manuel Carmona, "The Hairless Mexican," is an exiled revolutionary general with a specialty in assassinations, a mastery of disguises, and an enthusiasm for sexual conquests. Maugham based his character on that of an agent who worked with his friend the artist Sir Gerald Kelly, who served as an agent in Spain during the war. Unlike the Hairless Mexican, the original did not kill the wrong man but instead bolted during an assignment.

Two American characters, Wilbur Schäfer, ambassador to an unnamed country, and John Quincy Harrington, who conducts business in Russia, are Maugham's typical American males—extroverted, hearty, optimistic, self-assured, and talkative. They are recklessly courageous because they fail to perceive any danger exists. Discovering that the American ambassador is involved with a Swedish woman of uncertain loyalty, a wary Ashenden plants an agent in his household as a maid. Though he does not discover any breach of security, he learns of the American's revulsion against the icy formality and reserve of the British ambassador, Sir Herbert Witherspoon. By apprising Witherspoon of the problem, Ashenden contributes to a diminution of conflict between allies. Mr. Harrington, a New England Brahmin, disregards urgent warnings about danger in revolutionary Russia and, while going to retrieve his laundry, is shot by someone in a roving band of soldiers. Robert Calder has traced the source of "Mr. Harrington's Washing" to an anecdote from the memoirs of a Czech agent serving in Russia at the time.[23]

Ashenden represents the most fully realized form of the Maugham

45

persona, and his character is both well rounded and complex. Yet even though the collection bears his name and his role is unusually prominent for a Maugham persona, the stories belong primarily to the other characters. His role as writer serves as a convenient backdrop to the business at hand, but occasionally his inclination to create surfaces in the narratives. Once he sees a retired Irish colonel and his wife dining at an inn. As they leave, the old gentleman is delayed and his wife waits with resigned patience for him to open the door. The poignancy of the moment strikes Ashenden, for that one brief episode illuminates their whole life together: she has never before opened a door for herself. He could turn it into a story, but, he realizes, he has more pressing business. Ashenden's reflections on these two characters and his musing on creativity support Maugham's assertion that in his stories the character usually came first and the plot was created to fit the character.

It is easy to mistake Ashenden's careful control of emotion for the absence of emotion. About the control there can be no mistake. When he discovers that R has him under surveillance, he reacts only with amusement, not indignation. He loses his typical reserve only once, when he tells Manuel Carmona, "You bloody fool, you've killed the wrong man" (*Complete Stories*, vol. 1, 503). For the most part he remains coolheaded and analytical. When he perceives that Anastasia is not only intelligent but patriotic, he reflects that "like many patriots she had the impression that her own aggrandizement tended to the good of her country" (*Complete Stories*, vol. 1, 628), a comment that reflects his guarded view of human nature and his intelligence, not his lack of loyalty. The Maugham persona's skepticism calls attention to one of life's paradoxes, one that recurs in the fiction: that those who earnestly seek to do good, like the Reverend Mr. Davidson, often do the most harm.

Yet R mistakenly believes that Ashenden considers it all a game of chess, that he moves human beings as if they were pawns on a board, and Ashenden does not bother to correct the view. His unexpressed sentiment is suggested when he gazes on a bouquet of roses as R speaks. But repeatedly he shows compassion for the weak and empathy toward his enemies. The fullest description of his character occurs in "The Traitor":

> Ashenden admired goodness, but was not outraged by wickedness. People sometimes thought him heartless because he was more often interested in others than attached to them, and even in the few to whom he was attached his eyes saw with equal clearness the merits

and the defects. When he liked people it was not because he was blind
to their faults, he did not mind their faults but accepted them with a
tolerant shrug of the shoulders, or because he ascribed to them
excellencies that they did not possess; and since he judged his friends
with candour they never disappointed him and so he seldom lost one.
He asked from none more than he could give. (*Complete Stories*, vol. 1,
559)

To be sure, Ashenden is a fictional character, but the analytical,
tolerant observer of the passage, who expects little of human beings,
reflects the essential character and values of his creator. In a movie
version of a later Ashenden story, "Sanatorium," Maugham appeared on
screen to introduce the film and said to the audience, "If you like to take
the character of Ashenden as a flattering portrait of the old party who
stands before you, you are at perfect liberty to do so."[24] On the other
hand, Maugham reminds the reader in other contexts that the narrator-
persona is a character used for the sake of literary convention. If, as he
says, he sometimes makes the character wiser, wittier, and more percep-
tive than he, he also at other times makes the narrator more naive and
ingenuous than he.

The titles included in *Six Stories Written in the First Person Singular*
(1931), all with European settings, feature a Maugham persona who is
older and more worldly than his earlier versions. The collection resembles *Ashenden* in that both rely heavily on the Maugham persona, though
the third-person, named spokesman in *Ashenden* is replaced by the
first-person "I." A professional writer, he shows himself willing at times
to become involved in the difficulties encountered by his characters.
The characters and their stories are found in remote or out-of-the-way
settings, such as uncrowded resorts after the peak season. In their way
the characters are as exotic as those Maugham encountered during his
South Sea journeys. They exist on the fringes of society, or they are
caught in a time warp, appearing to belong to another age.

The narrator appears more interested in discussing his craft than
previously; one could glean most of Maugham's critical canons from two
of the stories, "The Human Element" and "The Creative Impulse." In
"The Human Element" the narrator dines alone in an almost deserted
hotel in Rome and begins to reflect on the writer's difficulty in describing a character so as to create in the reader's mind a clear and accurate
impression. He fixes his eye on a well-dressed gentleman seated nearby
and imagines how he would describe him. Recognizing the narrator as a
prominent writer, the guest invites him to share coffee in the lobby.

Belatedly, the narrator recognizes him as Humphrey Carruthers, a dip-
lomat and writer of short fiction. Increasingly in the later stories, the
narrator's role as an internationally known author makes him easily
recognizable, and in numerous stories he recalls someone he meets only
after the character has recognized him.

In a carefully crafted digression, he explains that Carruthers had
written two volumes that received acclaim from critics for their atmosphere, extremely limited point of view, and rich description. But they
were stories in which nothing much happened. In the best one a group of
characters left London for a weekend and resolved none of the problems
that arose during their country outing; on Monday they returned to their
urban existence with nothing changed. The narrator dismisses the story
of atmosphere for one with a beginning, middle, and end, and suggests
that stories like Humphrey's are destined for a short life. The section
clearly reflects Maugham's exasperation with highbrow critics who preferred the Chekhov type of story, just as the Ashenden stories set in
Russia reflect his impatience with the intelligentsia. To the highbrow
aesthete a story should create a mood through description at the expense
of narrative. To the intelligentsia the story should support a philosophical or political message. Maugham believes that a story should be
essentially a narrative intended to entertain, and the ironic conclusion of
"The Human Element" reinforces the narrator's point that Carruthers
does not recognize a story when he sees one.

When the two begin their coffee, Humphrey disconcerts the speaker,
whom he barely knows, by pronouncing, "I'm so unhappy." The narrator conceals his embarrassment, realizing Humphrey has a story to tell. It
is the story of his hapless but long-enduring love for Betty Welldon-
Burns, a debutante in London who had her fling after World War I. Her
high-spirited antics made her known to everyone in society until she
married James Welldon-Burns, the son of a wealthy manufacturer, and
settled on Rhodes. Although she rejected him, Humphrey's love for her
did not diminish with time, and they kept in touch through letters and an
occasional social meeting. Rumor spread that her husband had begun
drinking and they were separated. Eventually Humphrey read his obituary in the newspaper and, after waiting a discreet time, managed to
obtain from Betty an invitation to visit her at Rhodes.

At first the visit is successful, and Humphrey plans to propose to Betty
just before he departs. The climax occurs when he discovers, quite by
accident, that she has had a long-standing affair with her chauffeur.
Crushed by the revelation, Humphrey understands why Betty's hus-

band began drinking. His long-cherished ideal shattered, he is inclined to flee in panic, but on reflection decides he must do the noble thing and sacrifice himself to save her from the degrading life she has led. Though no longer in love with her, he proposes, and Betty politely refuses.

Instead of expressing astonishment or making a pointed query, the persona in the later stories more often seeks to say something that might be helpful. Having refrained from intervening during the story, he attempts to suggest a source of consolation. Writers, he tells Humphrey, have an advantage over other people in that they can shed their emotional burdens by writing stories about them. "It would be monstrous," Humphrey responds. "Besides, there's no story there."

The conflict between the highbrow and the commercial writer surfaces once again in "The Creative Impulse," another essentially literary tale. Comic episodes in the story border on the farcical, and the tone is ironic to the point of flippancy. Although the story is a first-person narrative, the persona appears seldom and takes no part in the plot. An infrequent guest at Mrs. Forrester's Tuesday-afternoon teas, he makes a sardonic joke on one occasion, but he influences neither the action nor the characters.

Mrs. Albert Forrester, a serious novelist and poet, holds a regular Tuesday salon for her highbrow friends in her fashionable London apartment near the Marble Arch. Although she has an enviable reputation as an artist, she must depend on her uninspired husband for support, since her books are not the kind people buy in quantity. Though he quietly assists her all he can, her friends find Albert dull, and someone labels him a philatelist. Since stamp collecting fits his personality, it becomes a standing joke. But humor changes to consternation when Albert elopes with Mrs. Bulfinch, the cook. Mrs. Forrester's agent persuades her to set aside her dignity and try to win him back, since his action makes her look too ridiculous for her books to sell at all. Albert refuses any reconciliation, but Mrs. Bulfinch offers the suggestion that Mrs. Forrester turn to detective fiction to supplement the £300 of support Albert will pay each year. After Mrs. Bulfinch explains that their mutual interest in detective stories had brought her and Albert together, Mrs. Forrester thinks the advice sensible. She informs her friends that she will turn her literary talent to detective fiction. Her first novel, *The Achilles Statue*, becomes a resounding commercial success.

The narrator plays a more substantial role in the remaining four stories, which represent a departure from the usual narrative technique. In "The Human Element" Maugham employed a narrative method that was foreshadowed in "The Punctiliousness of Don Sebastian" and developed fully through stories like "Good Manners," "Masterson," "Footprints in the Jungle," and "His Excellency." The narrator meets someone over dinner or at a bridge table. After everyone else has left, the other person, perhaps over brandy and cigars, bares his soul, telling a story with roots deep in the past. The narrator may or may not interject comments, but he plays a limited role in the remainder of the story.

By contrast, in four stories from *First Person Singular* the narrator meets different characters or groups who are brought together during the story and whose interactions form the plot. Because this narrative convention requires an extended period, the narrator enters and exits, sometimes over a span of years. The narrator's own experiences serve to bridge episodes spaced widely apart chronologically. A similar structural device occurs in novels like *The Razor's Edge* and *Cakes and Ale*.

The simplest story using this technique, "The Round Dozen," introduces Mortimer Ellis, whose character, by Maugham's own admission, was taken from life. Like others in the volume, he is exotic in his degree of departure from the norm. The setting is Elsom, a seedy and almost deserted English seaside resort, where the narrator has gone for a few days of rest. There he meets a London tea merchant, Edwin St. Clair; his wife, Gertrude; and their 54-year-old niece, Miss Porchester. They are exotic in time, for their dress, manners, and ethical attitudes reflect the high Victorian 1880s. Miss Porchester, who has a small inherited income, has remained unmarried after her betrothed of 30 years earlier was found unworthy because of an affair with the daughter of a laundress. When he subsequently married a socialite who did not seem to mind, Miss Porchester's exquisite moral sensitivity remained unaffected.

Mortimer Ellis, whom the narrator encounters on a park bench, is a far different kind of exotic. He has recently been released from prison, having completed a sentence for bigamy. He freely recounts his life story to the narrator, producing from his wallet faded newspaper articles about his notorious trial and conviction. Having been married 11 times, he now seeks to make it the round dozen, 11 being somehow incomplete. An accomplished confidence man, he uses almost identical methods in every case. At resorts he seeks out widows or spinsters between 35 and 50, courts them, and marries them in church. For a few months he assumes the role of model husband. Then, having secured their complete confidence, he tells them he can double their money in short order, takes everything they have, and disappears.

Since he has had such wide experience, he explains much about women and marriage to the narrator. His penchant for taking advantage of others is clarified by the way he extracts first cigarettes and then money from the narrator, who finds Ellis's lengthy account entertaining. The narrator sees Ellis for what he is but does not condemn him, for he recognizes that individuals, having been deprived of comforting grand illusions, must be permitted illusions about themselves. Ellis actually believes that the judge who sentenced him perpetrated an injustice, that his attentions to the neglected women were worth more to them than he gained through embezzling their savings.

When Miss Porchester mysteriously elopes, leaving behind a note hinting at her happiness, the St. Clairs approach the narrator, suggesting he might have had something to do with it. Knowing about Ellis, he grasps the truth at once and is able to assure them that she will certainly be married—in church.

"Jane," a sprightly story in the comedy-of-manners tradition, develops over a longer period than the two weeks required for "The Round Dozen." Mrs. Marian Tower, a London hostess, bemoans to the narrator the imminent visit of her provincial sister-in-law Jane Fowler, who must be entertained despite her innate plainness. But the next day she telephones to say that Jane is engaged to Gilbert Napier, 15 years her junior. Jane has rejected Mrs. Tower's well-intentioned warning that Gilbert will one day leave her for a younger woman and, though she is not in love with Gilbert, will marry him because she enjoys his attention. Shortly afterward the narrator leaves on a two-year journey to the Far East, the journey serving as a convenient bridge between two major episodes. On returning, he asks Mrs. Tower about the Napiers and learns Jane has been transformed into a stylish and witty woman in demand at London parties. Her success rests on her willingness to tell the truth, a quality that endows her with uniqueness in society. Gilbert has overseen her dress and appearance, much to the better, as the narrator discovers for himself when he attends one of Jane's parties. The tables have been turned on Mrs. Tower, but not for the final time. A second inversion occurs when news comes that the Napiers have separated and a disconsolate Gilbert informs Mrs. Tower that Jane has left him for an admiral her own age.

In "Virtue" and "The Alien Corn," two stories with more serious themes, the narrator finds himself more deeply involved in the plot. "Virtue" introduces an array of characters, beginning with Gerald Morton, whom the narrator encounters by chance on Bond Street. A figure from the narrator's past, an exotic returned to his original setting, Morton is a dedicated, conscientious resident in Borneo on leave in London with nothing to do. Since he had been the narrator's host, the narrator invites him to dine at his club, where they meet Charles and Margery Bishop, old friends of the narrator who have been married for a long time. Charles, a crusty pathologist, is no dancer, and Margery readily accepts Morton's invitation to dance. Thereafter the narrator departs on a trip and on his return discovers that Margery has fallen in love with Gerald. Although the two see each other constantly, they are strictly virtuous and Margery has told Charles everything. He considers it a huge joke that she should have fallen in love with a man so much younger. After his leave ends, Gerald returns to Borneo, and Margery, unable to bear her husband's ridicule, leaves him. She explains that she will go to Borneo and marry Gerald after divorcing Charlie. Jane, a mutual friend, offers lodging to Margery when they are first separated and then to Charlie after Margery has found a place of her own. Charlie begins drinking heavily, and when he fails to appear at a dinner scheduled with the narrator, it is discovered that he has committed suicide. From Borneo Gerald cables his condolence to Margery and tells her a letter is on its way. When the letter arrives, it dashes her hopes by explaining all the reasons she should not come to the colony.

To Jane the narrator explains that virtue was the entire problem: if the two had had their affair, it would have ended; instead, they have been virtuous and truthful and have caused death and unhappiness. Jane is shocked by the cynicism and insists that the narrator, who introduced Margery and Gerald, persuade Gerald to do the right thing. This he wholly rejects, and they part with recrimination. The story develops Maugham's paradoxical theme, beginning with "Daisy" and expressed in its starkest terms in "The Judgment Seat," that conventional ideas of virtue often result in greater harm than vice.

"The Alien Corn" introduces another category of exotic characters, Jews living in English society. It begins with a depiction of one of Maugham's most memorable characters, Ferdy Rabenstein, an affluent, sociable, irrepressible London bachelor, well advanced in years, who, like the narrator, is an unabashed hedonist. Ferdy is popular at parties, where he entertains guests by playing the piano and telling Jewish stories with gusto. Also like the narrator, he is something of a *raisonneur*, taking little part in the action. From Ferdy the narrator learns, much to his surprise, that the Blands, who have invited the narrator to their country estate, are his relatives.

Sir Adolphous Bland, Ferdy's nephew, is a member of Parliament and cabinet officer. His wife, Muriel, and their two sons, George and Harry, live conventional English upper-class lives, avoiding all Jewish ties—familial (Ferdy included), social, and cultural. Muriel has converted to Catholicism, and the two sons are given strictly English educations at the best schools. The family changed their name from the German Bleikogal to Bland during World War I, following the lead of the royal family and many other aristocrats with German names. They expect that George, who has been sent down from Oxford for idling, will inherit the estate and lead a distinguished political career. No one bothers to ask George's preference in the matter.

As the narrator discovers, more than anything else George wants to become a concert pianist. Although he persuades his parents to send him to Munich to study German, he goes in reality to study music. A family crisis develops when he returns for his twenty-first birthday celebration and announces that instead of beginning a political career, he will return to Munich. His enraged father cuts him off and creates a scene; only Lady Hannah Bland, the matriarch and grandmother, can settle the matter. She persuades George to give himself two years to decide whether his talent is adequate, and to agree to abandon his ambition if it isn't. She will pay his expenses and no one in the family will bother him. This final provision leads to an encounter between George and the narrator, since Muriel wants news of her son, and so the narrator pays a visit while he is traveling on other matters.

He finds George among Jewish artists and intellectuals, leading a Bohemian life. George works seriously at his piano lessons, but the narrator (an amateur pianist) notices that something in his technique is flawed. In his later report to Muriel, the narrator omits troubling details like these.

When George returns after two years for an assessment and judgment by Lea Makart, the consummate artist, the narrator is on hand. He grows somewhat uneasy when he hears her pronouncing, without qualification, that people are only the artist's raw material, and art is all that matters, opinions he himself has uttered but clearly does not entirely accept. She patiently listens to George's playing, and then, in response to the inevitable question about his prospects as a pianist, replies, "Never in a thousand years." Recognizing his pain, she offers to obtain for George a hearing from Paderewski, but he declines, saying her judgment confirms what he already thought. Sir Adolphous offers to grant George more time or send him around the world, but George asks only to take a walk. Instead, he goes to the gun room and puts a bullet through his heart.

The reader might expect that, thematically, the story would concern itself with assimilation in a modern nation-state. In reality this theme serves only to provide contrasting points of view and minor conflicts among the characters. Running throughout the works of Maugham, like a thread, is an almost fatalistic view that human beings cannot really escape their genetic and cultural background. Maugham doubted, for example, whether Americans who wanted to understand England and the English ever really could. Had the Blands not been so keen on assimilation, they might have recognized George's true ambition sooner and viewed it more sympathetically.

The more important theme is the appeal of aesthetic creativity and its effects on characters, a theme developed in various ways in Maugham's fiction. Maugham himself fully recognized that art is not all that matters, although he found in great artistic achievement an extenuation of personal failings. But he knew aesthetic individuals for whom only art mattered, and created characters with similar values. In *Of Human Bondage*, Philip Carey has the strength to abandon his ambition of becoming a painter after he recognizes he will never be more than mediocre. On the other hand, Fanny Price, finding nothing else in life meaningful, is destroyed by her unrealistic ambition to become an artist. In the obscure story "The Buried Talent," the heroine eventually commits suicide after missing her chance for a career as a concert singer. And in *The Moon and Sixpence*, Charles Strickland throws over a successful career and abandons his family in order to become an artist. Because his talent is genuine, he finds partial justification for what he has done.

Cosmopolitans: The Short Shorts

In the preface to *Cosmopolitans*, Maugham explains that its 29 stories were written between 1923 and 1929 for *Cosmopolitan* magazine. The magazine's editor, Ray Long, favorably impressed by two stories in Maugham's volume of travel literature *On a Chinese Screen*, invited him to write similar ones suitable for the magazine. Except for a few titles in the *Ashenden* collection, the stories are shorter than the earlier ones, running from under 2,000 to approximately 4,000 words. They include less description of setting and character than the earlier stories; they avoid long, leisurely exposition; and their conclusions seem more striking and perhaps more strained. Compared with the better-known South Sea stories, the reversals occur more abruptly and the irony seems starker. In a few, "A Friend in Need" being a prominent example, the cynical tone stands out in sharp relief. In the preface Maugham makes the mistake that many writers fall into when describing their own work. Despite his awareness that a man of letters should leave behind a solid legacy, he candidly admits that the stories were written only for entertainment and thus hands critics ammunition to use against him.

The settings reflect the variety usually encountered in a Maugham collection. The most straightforward and conventional stories are set in England, but one also finds Italian, Spanish, South Sea, Russian, Latin American, and Asiatic settings. A recurring theme in those with exotic settings is that of a character who finds either happiness and fulfillment or destruction in new surroundings. Typically, the protagonists have been away from their homelands for many years. In "Mayhew" a Detroit lawyer becomes enchanted with Capri and moves to the island. There he experiences happiness, even though he dies before writing his projected history of the island. Similarly, in "The Happy Man" a physician leaves London for practice in Spain, where he experiences a rewarding life. Meeting him by chance and without recognition, the narrator learns from the doctor how he happened to be living in Spain. Years earlier, while they were medical students together in London, the narrator advised him to follow his inclination to settle abroad. The grateful physician asserts that he has lived better than kings. "In a Strange Land" depicts an Englishwoman successfully earning her living by running a small hotel in Asia Minor.

By contrast, "German Harry" and "French Joe" explore the narrator's encounter with two Europeans who discovered that the freedom offered by life in the South Seas brought them only degradation and misfortune. A slight variation of this theme occurs when the narrator combines it with the theme of the failed artist. In "The Bum" he is struck by the appearance of a Vera Cruz beggar and on their second meeting remembers him as a young artist in Rome. Completely destitute and uncommunicative, he is beyond the help of the narrator or anyone else. In one futile, defiant gesture, he rolls a dollar bill the narrator has given him into a tight ball and flips it to clamorous vultures.

Several stories in the collection rely heavily on literary sources. "Mr. Know-All" and "A String of Beads" offer variations on the theme originally found in Maupassant's "The Necklace." "The Ant and the Grasshopper" draws an analogy to the fable by La Fontaine. In "The Wash Tub" the speaker is amused by Mrs. Barnaby's success in London society, since her secret lies in appealing to the English romantic temperament by telling stories of the American frontier derived from Bret Harte and presenting them as her own experiences. But among this literary group, "The Portrait of a Gentleman" is the most instructive, for it demonstrates Maugham's ingenuity at constructing a story from an unpromising source.

The title appears to cast the story as an ironic sequel to Henry James's *The Portrait of a Lady*. In a Seoul bookshop the narrator discovers a well-worn book entitled *The Complete Poker-Player*, by John Blackbridge, and buys it for a pittance. He gives an account of the book at the beginning, almost as if writing a review. Gradually the narrator evokes the author's character by centering on his interests and style. Like the narrator, Blackbridge has read La Rouchefoucauld and is fond of maxims. Selecting primarily those which point up the author's gentility, the narrator proceeds to quote maxims and words of advice from the book, some about poker playing but others about life in general. Their tone of civilized restraint can be gathered from an example dealing with emotional responses to good and bad fortune at cards: "To feel emotions over such incidents is unworthy of a man; and it is much more unworthy to express them. But no words need be wasted over practices which all men despise in others; and, in their reflecting moments, lament in themselves" (*Complete Stories*, vol. 2, 159). The narrator finds irony in the fact that a writer of a somewhat technical book on poker should uphold the code of a gentleman. Clearly, he admires the combination of intelligence, worldly realism, keen analytical ability, and sense of honor the writer displays. Occasionally he acknowledges that, as a player, he has not always lived up to the code Blackbridge insists on, thus contrasting himself with the author. The story concludes with a series of Blackbridge maxims that the narrator finds witty and enlightening.

The remarkable thing about this story is that the book exists,[25] and the quotations, forming more than half of the text, are usually copied verbatim, as the story suggests. The final quoted aphorism, one Maugham adopts as his own and uses elsewhere, is "For we must take human nature as it is."[26] Even when the narrator discovers a kindred soul, however, it is useful for him to contrast that person with himself, and he shows no reluctance in portraying Blackbridge as the better gentlemen.

In several of the stories, the narrator is willing to acknowledge his mistakes in order to create effective suspense. The reader normally identifies with the first-person speaker, and when the speaker shows himself to be naive or fallible, the ironic conclusion is enhanced. It must be noted that the ironic reversals in several stories are so abrupt as to seem contrived. In "Raw Material" the narrator undercuts the argument that characters are created from real life. Aboard a steamer bound from Hong Kong to New York, he identifies two fellow passengers as cardsharpers, even though one claims to be an engineer and the other a banker. All of their actions on board confirm his conclusion. Later he meets them by chance at a party in New York and discovers they really are an engineer and a banker.

A second example of mistaken identity occurs when the narrator visits an aged Spanish poet in his native city. Bearing a letter of introduction, he is introduced to the poet and is almost overcome by the aura of dignity that surrounds him, a dignity created not only by the poet's appearance but by the romantic associations inherent in his poetry. The narrator's awestruck feeling is utterly deflated when he discovers that he has come to the wrong apartment, that the man before him is in truth a retired bristle merchant. In a similar story offering a heavy-handed conquest of romanticism by realism, "The Man with the Scar," the narrator meets a Nicaraguan whose forehead is graced with a disfiguring scar and assumes the explanation of its origin to be heroic exploits. From an account of man's past, the narrator does learn of a romantic and violent story of danger and death, but his assumption about the scar is ironically undermined: the man received it from an exploding bottle of soda water. Like

Miss Ley in "The Happy Couple," the narrator discovers that reality dispels romantic illusions.

"Mr. Know-All," a complex story of this kind, features a more subtle reversal. Boarding a steamer in San Francisco, the narrator discovers he must share his cabin with a stranger. He prefers a peaceful, quiet voyage, alleviated with a game of patience when boredom sets in. His cabin companion, Max Kelada, a pearl merchant, is the kind of character the reserved narrator instantly dislikes—garrulous, self-assured, ingratiating, presumptuous, and, above all, boring. His self-centered conversation suggests he is an authority on all subjects. Dining in company one evening, he identifies a pearl necklace on a passenger as of great worth. The necklace belongs to Mrs. Ramsey, a woman from New York whose husband has recently rejoined her after serving a year on a diplomatic mission. Mr. Ramsey, who, like the narrator, bridles at Kelada's confident speech, scoffs at the idea, asserting that his wife recently bought the pearls at a department store for a few dollars. After they place bets on their respective positions, Kelada inspects the pearls under a magnifying glass. As he prepares to announce his victory, he perceives an expression of panic on Mrs. Ramsey's face. An instant later he pronounces them false and hands over a hundred dollar bill to the exultant Ramsey. The next morning a mysterious envelope appears under the cabin door, and Kelada finds a hundred dollar bill inside. "If I had a pretty wife I shouldn't let her spend a year in New York while I stayed at Kobe" (*Complete Stories*, vol. 2, 148), he casually remarks. The real story, one of an extramarital affair, has remained untold, and the narrator acknowledges that he must change his opinion of Kelada.

The central anecdote of "A Friend in Need" establishes Maugham's most cynical tone. The story begins simply with the narrator reflecting on the art of writing. He observes that the most artificial facet of fiction arises from the writer's need to create characters that are consistent, in order to ensure the suspension of disbelief, whereas real human beings, not being all of a piece, are riddled with contradictions. The story of Edward Hyde Burton, whose obituary the narrator has just read, illustrates Maugham's main point.

The narrator recalls a bridge game with Burton at the British Club in Yokohama. Burton, a British merchant from Kobe, was known as a devoted husband and father, a man with a reputation of unfailing kindness toward others. After the game Burton narrates the story of Lenny Burton, who lost everything through drinking and gambling and applied to him for a job, perhaps because their family names were identical.

When he unexpectedly learned his namesake was good at swimming, he offered a job on the condition that Lenny swim a perilous course along the shoreline. Though physically unfit for the ordeal, Lenny accepted out of desperation and failed to reach his destination, where the employer was to meet him. At the end the narrator intervenes by asking, "When you made him that offer of a job, did you know he'd be drowned?" and Burton responds, "Well, I hadn't got a vacancy in my office at the moment" (*Complete Stories*, vol. 2, 169). The story reflects a cynicism about human nature that influenced John Whitehead to designate a few of Maugham's later stories as "rancid."[27]

Especially in anecdotes from *A Writer's Notebook* that were not used for stories, it is obvious that Maugham was sometimes drawn to truly sordid aspects of human nature. Yet cynicism is not all the story reflects: besides being a well-told tale, it demonstrates, largely through the narrative voice, Maugham's intense and genuine interest in human nature.

In "Louise" the plot suggests that the narrator's advice is mistaken but not necessarily wrong. Whereas in "The Happy Man" his cautious and reluctant advice to the young physician to go to Spain had turned out well, in "Louise" his calculated, deliberate intervention produces mixed results at best. Louise, a London socialite, has known the narrator for many years, and neither bothers to conceal their mutual dislike. She has complained of some mysterious illness for most of her life, but luckily she found two husbands eager to devote themselves to her care. One exhausted himself and died; the other had been killed in the war. She now has only her daughter Iris to take care of her. Louise finds it natural that her mature daughter should devote her entire life to her, and when Iris receives an offer of marriage, Louise reminds her of her obligation. Saying that she knows the marriage will be her death, Louise effectively forestalls any separate life for Iris.

At this point the narrator intervenes, telling Louise that there is nothing wrong with her and she should not prevent Iris from leading her own life. She replies that although it will kill her (and then the narrator will be sorry), she will agree to the marriage. The story quickly chronicles details leading up to the ceremony, until the indignant narrative voice abruptly turns to the wedding morning: "On the wedding-day at ten o'clock in the morning, Louise, that devilish woman, had one of her heart attacks—and died" (*Complete Stories*, vol. 2, 534). Far from acknowledging his error about her condition, the narrator leaves the impression that she timed her death so as to create the greatest harm.

Among the stories set in England, "The Escape" represents a farcical avoidance of marriage by an unwilling groom and "The Ant and the Grasshopper" finds the narrator laughing without restraint at its conclusion because a totally irresponsible brother had better fortune than the responsible one who tells the story. "The Promise" and "The Social Sense" develop Maugham's theme of extramarital affairs and the fragility of relationships, these being particularly mellow and poignant examples. "Home" recounts the return of England of a colonial official, who dies shortly after his arrival.

"The Verger," a story of gentle charm and irony, is arguably the best of *Cosmopolitans* and is among the best known. Albert Edward Foreman, the verger at St. Peter's Church, Neville Square, carries out his duties with a dignity and expertise acquired through 16 years of service. But when the new vicar discovers that he can neither read nor write, and is unwilling to learn, he forces Albert to resign. The verger, at a loss for something to do, goes for a walk in search of a tobacco shop. When he realizes that he has to walk a long way to find one, it occurs to him that opening a shop along the street he chose might prove successful. He leases space with his savings and opens a tobacco shop; when it succeeds, he opens others as well. Within 10 years he owns 10 successful shops, and his banker, impressed by the size of his account, takes him aside to suggest a favorable investment. When he discovers Albert can neither read nor write, he asks, "What would you be now if you'd been able to?" (*Complete Stories*, vol. 2, 578). Albert, who finds the question easy, replies that he would be the verger at St. Peter's, Neville Square.

The stories reveal additional facts about the narrator, and often the details are biographically correct for Maugham. In "The Promise" the narrator acknowledges that he is married to an unpunctual wife, who fails to show up for a luncheon appointment, thus giving him an unexpected opportunity to dine with another woman and hear her story. In "The End of the Flight," the narrator gives a hint of the Maugham stammer after learning that he is to sleep in a bed whose previous occupant was murdered in his sleep. "The Luncheon," a second version of "Cousin Amy," demonstrates the narrator's use of time to create an effective ending. Meeting his partner 20 years after the luncheon, he recalls the story essentially as it happened in the original, except that the setting is Paris rather than London. All of his original chagrin at the meal's expense and details of its impact on his straitened budget are preserved, but the older narrator concludes that he has at last had his revenge, because she weighs three hundred pounds. Stories like "The Luncheon" and "Louise" support the critical opinion, often expressed, that Maugham's attitude toward women is ungallant, but one could cite numerous others that cast their heroines in a favorable light.

As in earlier stories, references to the narrator as a writer are common. In "The Promise" Lady Elizabeth Vermont reminds the narrator that as a novelist he should understand something about human nature. But in "Salvatore" Maugham does something with the writer's persona that he later expanded in *The Razor's Edge*: he attempts to involve the reader in the process of writing by describing the challenge he sees before him while producing the work. *The Razor's Edge* begins with the arresting sentence "I have never begun a novel with more misgiving,"[28] letting the reader assume that the speaker is beginning his work with apprehension and attempting to involve the reader in the process of creation. "Salvatore" opens with a similar note of apprehension: "I wonder if I can do it" (*Complete Stories*, vol. 2, 263). The story then develops a character sketch of an Italian fisherman the narrator claims to have known for a decade or more. The final paragraph ends the suspense by explaining what it was he was trying to do—to describe goodness, simple goodness. The story is atypical in its portrayal of an entirely flawless character.

The Mixture as Before and Creatures of Circumstance

Maugham's final two volumes of stories published during his lifetime, *The Mixture as Before* (1940) and *Creatures of Circumstance* (1947), include 25 titles, most of them written during the 1930s and 1940s. Exceptions are "The Happy Couple" and "The Mother," both revisions of stories written and published before 1910. Like those in *Cosmopolitans*, the stories in the two final volumes are extremely varied, but they contain little by way of new directions. Their settings are ones found previously—Spain, France, the Riviera, the South Seas, England, Scotland, Capri, Latin America, and the United States. Stories from these volumes, along with those in *Cosmopolitans*, formed the second and final volume of the collected edition, entitled *The World Over* (1952). The first, *East and West* (1934), offered 30 titles from the South Sea collections, *Ashenden*, and *First Person Singular*. In addition to stories from the three final volumes, *The World Over* includes 7 titles previously published in magazines or in the travel books but omitted from any previous collection.

The title of the earlier volume is ironic, for an anonymous reviewer for the London *Times* entitled his article on *Cosmopolitans* "Mr. Maugham's Mixture as Before." The phrase, used at that time for reordering a supply of pipe tobacco, was intended as an unfavorable tag, and the reviewer concluded that the collection would not add to the author's reputation. Maugham used the review title for his next collection, arguing in his preface that an artist's contribution stems from a unique individuality—the artist's vision, attitudes, and values. It is a view of the artist he elaborates on elsewhere and one reflecting his principle that every life forms a unique pattern. The title *Creatures of Circumstance* reflects Maugham's conception of character. On one level it indicates he is viewing all his major characters as exotic, akin to those who were molded by their remote environments. On a second and more fundamental level, it reveals his deterministic conviction that character develops from the genetic and environmental circumstances that influence it.

From the character and themes, one finds little that is new in the two volumes. The unfaithful wife, the hushed up scandal that comes to light in time, the exile who finds happiness or despair, the disastrous passion, the drawing room comedy, the crime of violence, the artist's life—all are found in these stories. Yet Maugham also includes tales of abnormal psychology, a theme not without precedent but definitely uncommon in his earlier fiction. One story from *On a Chinese Screen*, "The Taipan," represents an early example of a tale of psychological terror. "Lord Mountdrago" recounts a political rivalry, exacerbated by social differences between rivals, that is accompanied by the hero's guilt-hidden dreams and results in the strange deaths of both. In "A Man from Glasgow," the narrator meets a Scot in Spain who tells the story of hearing demonic laughter during each full-moon night and discomfits the narrator by pointing out that the evening of their meeting marks the full moon. "The Kite" explores a young man's obsessive fascination with kites and its deleterious effects on his marriage. A single story from *Creatures of Circumstance*, "The Unconquered," breaks new thematic ground. Written during World War II, it deals with the lives of French peasants under German occupation. It recalls somewhat the tone of Maupassant's stories set during the Franco-Prussian War and the Prussian occupation. Despite its tragic theme, the story appears to be primarily an effort at propaganda and is not among Maugham's most successful.

In narrative technique the two volumes reveal only a gradual shift from stories of the earlier periods. Many are written in the familiar third-person omniscient, including some of the better-known ones like "The Colonel's Lady" and "Winter Cruise." In those featuring the Maugham persona, the narrator has aged and mellowed, so that he becomes even more reticent about offering advice or involving himself in the action. In several stories time creates distance from the action. In "The Romantic Young Lady," a humorous Spanish story, the narrator reflects on the advantages of growing old: "Sometimes it gives you the opportunity of seeing what was the outcome of certain events you had witnessed long ago" (*Complete Stories*, vol. 2, 313). What follows is a story, like several others set in the past, introducing a protagonist the narrator had known; in this case the heroine had been the narrator's dancing partner 40 years earlier. In more than one story, the narrator meets without recognition someone from his past who knows him. Gradually he recalls their earlier meetings, and the character's story unfolds. The story may entertain, but distance in time and the narrator's own lack of recognition leave the reader minimally involved with the characters. But however reluctant he may be to intervene or advise, the narrator freely offers his judgments and interpretations to the reader. Instead of relying on a philosophical doctor, a crusty and worldly-wise sea captain, or an enlightened administrator, the narrator at times becomes the *raisonneur* and interprets, as if recalling his role in "Virtue."

"The Lotus Eater," yet another story featuring the theme of a character enchanted with an exotic setting, demonstrates how the narrator obtains knowledge of the story over time and how time does its work. In 1913 he visits Capri and meets Tom Wilson, who has been there for 15 years. On his first visit at age 35, Wilson was so enchanted with the island that he decided to quit his routine job, invest all of his assets in a 25-year annuity, and come there to live. When his money ran out at age 60, he planned to commit suicide, after spending a quarter-century of blissful independence. Thirteen years after he first learns about Wilson, the narrator returns to Capri and asks about him. He discovers that when Wilson's deadline arrived, his nerve failed, and he began to borrow. After being evicted from his house, he attempted suicide, and the botched effort left his mind impaired. When the narrator again sees him, Wilson acts more like a wild animal than a man. After living 6 years in this condition, he dies, having lived a hedonistic existence that, after all, did not satisfy.

In "A Casual Affair" the narrator blends the themes of failure in an exotic setting and failure in a romantic relationship. Meeting Arthur Low and his wife in London, he recalls visiting Low in Borneo, where he was a district officer. The Lows mention two other mutual acquaintances, Jack Almond, a recently deceased colonial, and Lady Kastellan, a prominent London hostess. They explain how Almond died of opium addiction after spending several years in Borneo. Almond's physical condition had declined to the point that when Low was called to investigate his death, he could not recognize him. Following the dead man's written directions, Low delivered a packet of letters and an expensive cigarette case to Lady Kastellan. The letters revealed most but not all of the story. After a passionate affair with Lady Kastellan, Jack Almond had been forced to leave his Foreign Office job and go to the colonies. He expected her to abandon her husband and join him, but she refused. The narrator explains the effects of misplaced idealism: "He'd sacrificed everything, his friends, his familiar surroundings, his profession, his usefulness in the world, all that gives value to existence—for nothing. He'd been cheated, and it broke him" (*Complete Stories*, vol. 2, 140).

The theme of failed love leading to tragedy recurs in "Flotsam and Jetsam," a grim story set in Borneo; "A Woman of Fifty"; and "Episode," one of Maugham's final stories. For the most part, however, the later stories reflect Maugham's view that failed love, particularly that involving infidelity, is a subject for comedy rather than tragedy. "The Treasure" recounts the brief, indiscreet involvement of a dapper Home Office official with his excellent parlormaid following an evening together at the theater. Troubled with the thought that he will have to dismiss her, he finds her going about her work the next day as though nothing had happened and concludes with relief that he can safely retain the best parlormaid in London. The sense of class distinction and of a carefully structured society insulates the characters from the emotional consequences of their indiscretions. "The Romantic Young Lady" recounts the love affair between a Spanish debutante and the coachman of her mother's principal social rival. The mother is led to swallow her pride and ask her rival for help, and the affair is discreetly ended. "Appearance and Reality," set in France, portrays the affair between a French senator and a fashion model, Lisette, who becomes his mistress. In a scene bordering on farce, the aged senator arrives at her apartment unexpectedly and finds Lisette in bed with a young man. Lisette summons all her charm and ingenuity to bring about a resolution that satisfies everyone involved.

The most significant of these comical treatments of the love theme is "The Colonel's Lady," set in prewar England. Narrated entirely in the third person, it includes highly effective dramatic encounters. In the preface to volume 3 of the Heinemann edition, Maugham writes that his last story was composed in 1945 and based on an anecdote from his journal dated 1901. Although he does not mention a title, "The Colonel's Lady" appears to be the story, for *A Writer's Notebook* includes among selections from 1901 the brief anecdotal basis of its plot: "They were talking about V.F. whom they'd all known. She published a volume of passionate love poems, obviously not addressed to her husband. It made them laugh to think that she'd carried on a long affair under his nose, and they'd have given anything to know what he felt when at last he read them" (*Notebook*, 76).

The story introduces two mismatched middle-aged people, George and Eve Peregrine, who together run a country estate. The third-person narrative shifts gradually into the characters' point of view, a device Maugham uses chiefly with male characters and almost invariably with comic irony. The Peregrines live routinely enough until the normal serenity is broken by Evie's publication, under her maiden name, E. K. Hamilton, of a small volume of poems entitled *Though Pyramids Decay*. She gives her bluff, hearty husband, whose characterization borders on caricature, a copy at the breakfast table, and, puzzled by the publication, he takes the volume to his study. During a cursory examination he discovers that some poems are not rhymed and others have lines of irregular length, not his idea of poetry. Though relieved to find that one poem, entitled "Sonnet," has 14 lines, he lays the book aside, tells his wife he enjoyed it, and goes about his normal business.

Here the story might have ended, except that the book becomes an unanticipated commercial success. George Peregrine hears phrases like "Hot stuff" applied to the contents and vaguely senses that people are laughing at him when he attends receptions for Evie. Deciding he must read the book, he buys a copy for himself and discovers that the poems narrate the story of a secret love affair between a middle-aged woman and a young man who died unexpectedly after a few months. Realizing the story is autobiographical, he appeals to his lawyer for advice on how to proceed. With the injured husband presenting his side, the experienced and wise lawyer provides balance and a reasoned approach. He convinces George that the best course is to do nothing. It is a recurrence of Maugham's earlier theme that "the right thing is the kind thing," except that the story makes plain that the kind thing is also in the colonel's own interest.

In "The Voice of the Turtle," Maugham expands the literary element and makes use of the narrator as the main contrasting character. Just as Maugham employs two different personalities to create tension in "The Colonel's Lady," he uses the Maugham persona in a similar role in "The Voice of the Turtle," employing literary taste as the principal contrasting theme. The narrator is invited to a party in Bloomsbury, given in honor of the young highbrow novelist Peter Melrose. Although he dislikes Melrose, he is touched when the young author presents him with an autographed copy of his latest novel. He decides to invite Melrose to visit his home on the Riviera, and Melrose accepts. During the visit the narrator learns Melrose is writing a novel portraying a prima donna, and, seeking to be helpful, he invites a real-life prima donna, La Falterona, to dinner. While the narrative unmasks her as conceited, garrulous, and obtuse, Melrose is smitten by her charm. The observant, realistic narrator analyzes with a cold eye what escapes the wistful idealism of Melrose.

Later La Falterona meets the narrator and complains about Melrose's novel, a book that was not successful. She shows her usual crassness and conceit, but is then persuaded to sing. She does a shattering rendition of a poignant work by Maugham's favorite composer, the *Liebestodt* from *Tristan und Isolde*. Wryly acknowledging her triumph, the narrator comments, "She was hateful, of course, but she was irresistible."

The final Ashenden story, "Sanatorium," is based on Maugham's own experience in a tuberculosis sanatorium in Scotland in 1918 and indicates his inclination in the later stories to use materials from a much earlier time. Offering enough characters and themes for a novel, the story seeks to re-create life in the closed and sheltered environment of an institution where petty rivalries, animosities, and jealousies, exacerbated by inevitable gossip, are the rule. Yet it shows human nature rising above these through more serious pursuits. Unlike some of the other patients, Ashenden is not critically ill, and therefore he can offer comfort to others and insight to the reader. The narrative is exceptionally rich in characterization for a Maugham story, featuring three important couples and several minor characters. The strong animosity between two old residents serves to keep both alive, until one of them unexpectedly dies. The death appears to influence two other characters, Major Templeton and the frail, beautiful Evie Bishop, to marry and leave the sanatorium, even though their doctor has assured them that the change will shorten their lives. Following their marriage, a third pair, Henry Chester and his devoted wife, who visits from time to time, find a more peaceful relationship because Chester is able to come to terms with the reality that he will die while she will live. Maugham skillfully weaves the strands of the plot, interspersing it with Ashenden's philosophical perspective, so that the story possesses a thematic richness unusual for a short story.

"Episode" and "The Kite," among the last stories Maugham wrote, were suggested by Alan Searle, Maugham's longtime secretary, who heard the original versions while serving as a prison visitor. In the stories Searle appears as Ned Preston, the narrator's mild-mannered, sympathetic friend, who had visited prisoners in Wormwood Scrubbs Prison to provide company and to bear messages to their friends and relatives. In "Episode," a story making use of a frame, Ned tells a group of people the story of a rogue sent to prison for mail theft, and his devoted fiancée, who awaits his release. He gets a laugh from the group by concluding the story with the prisoner's falling out of love in prison, but saves the tragic conclusion for only the narrator: the comedy of a failed relationship preceded the tragic suicide of the prisoner's devoted fiancée.

In "The Kite" the narrator begins seemingly aimless reflections about psychology and then shifts to describing a leisurely dinner with Ned

Preston. Over brandy and cigars, Ned tells the story of a prisoner who chooses to remain in jail rather than pay court-ordered support to the estranged wife who broke his kite. The incredulous narrator then retells Ned's account of the Sunbury family, an ordinary family of three with an overly protective mother, a timid father, and a son of seeming average ability. Able to afford only simple pleasures, they cherish their hobby of flying kites on Sunday afternoons. Abundant details make what seemed incredible more understandable, for the major conflict arises when the young Herbert Sunbury must choose between his kite and his young wife. The narrator's voice at the end attempts to suggest the psychological importance of the kite to the commonplace protagonist.

Conclusion

In assessing his own career, Maugham wrote that he belonged not in the first rank of writers but at the head of the second rank, and, like many of his other critical pronouncements, this one appears on target. For one to attain a place among the greatest authors, prolific and prolonged literary production is not sufficient. The greatest artists must have at least some claim to altering their chosen literary forms, a claim that cannot be sustained for Maugham. Essentially he was a traditionalist who made no attempt to alter the narrative form of the short story. The same limitation applies to his novels and dramas; one critic has characterized *Of Human Bondage* as the greatest nineteenth-century novel written in the twentieth century.[29]

Further, as even sympathetic critics like Richard Cordell have pointed out, Maugham might have achieved a more substantial reputation as a serious artist had he explored the human psyche more deeply. He witnessed the origin and development of depth psychology and psychoanalysis but only peripherally explored their value for illuminating the human psyche. In most of his fiction, the novels *Of Human Bondage* and *The Razor's Edge* being exceptions, Maugham resembles authors like Chaucer, Dryden, Congreve, Voltaire, Pope, and Balzac, in that his works lack what Matthew Arnold called "high seriousness." Essentially a storyteller in the manner of Maupassant, he let the characters' external appearance, words, and actions illuminate their souls.

As for the depths of the human soul, Maugham's view of humanity was shaped by his medical training and science, especially by his reading of Darwin, and his expectations for human kind were modest. Not one to take what Coleridge termed the high road to humanity, he did not flinch from the pessimistic view that life is without meaning, and confessed difficulty in separating the concept of soul from its physical basis. If Ernest Hemingway can be considered a realist in the romantic tradition, Maugham represents a realist in the classical tradition. His view of literature as a profession, his sense of tradition and form, his fondness for aphorisms, and his fundamental distrust of emotion indicate his affinities with classicism. His basic metaphor for human life was the pattern, but he candidly acknowledged that even if one succeeds in making a coherent pattern of life, the achievement has no significance beyond itself. He rejected the idea that suffering ennobles, a concept vital to tragedy, and argued against it as a damaging illusion of the past. Viewing the human condition as inherently comic, he sought to explore the ironies of human nature rather than to celebrate the potential nobility of human beings.

He equally ignored the political and intellectual movements of the world at large, at least during peacetime. He wrote in a time when novelists like Aldous Huxley, George Orwell, and Arthur Koestler were exploring serious social and political themes and thereby finding a niche in the intellectual movements of the time. Maugham clearly rejected the idea of the artist as social reformer, and he considered works that brought social consciousness to the fore to be lightweight and propagandistic. For the most part he was correct on the point, for art with a message is not easily distinguished from propaganda, and, however successful with contemporaries, it seldom wears well. This is not to say that Maugham ignored reform altogether, but even in stories where it appears as a theme he presents it as secondary. As a Darwinian he embraced the idea of progress, yet he thought it desirable for one to accept humanity's insignificant place in the meaningless universe that science so starkly portrayed. A committed realist, he believed humanity needed to be liberated from many cruel illusions of the past and sought at times to contribute to the end.

In "The Point of Honour," the narrator-persona hears a Spanish story of a duel. For a trivial slight a young soldier is forced to accept a duel with a master, a choice that makes his death inevitable. The person who recounts the story, the narrator suspects, is the one who issued the challenge. "Barbarous . . . it was just cold-blooded murder" (*Complete Stories*, vol. 2, 298), the narrator responds, and yet he permits the Spanish speaker the final view of codes of honor.

Despite his profound pessimism, Maugham is a moralist who advocates ethical principles, modest though they are. Although he develops no coherent ethical system, he clearly upholds two primary virtues: tolerance and kindness, in that order. Beyond these he proposes a restrained civility, a sense of good form, as desirable in human life and society. He believes that on the whole, life goes better when individuals forgive slights instead of nursing grievances. Implicit in much of his fiction is an almost classical emphasis on the need to keep emotion under control. Essentially a hedonist, he has no objection to pleasure, but at the same time he believes in—and practiced—an ethic of work.

A consummate craftsman, Maugham produced highly readable stories. His mastery of colloquial expression, his sense of dramatic conflict, and his careful attention to plot and structure establish him as an undisputed master of the well-made narrative. While critics have at times condemned his clichés and colloquial language, careful examination of the stories reveals that usually the offending passages are spoken by characters for whom they are appropriate. Among Maugham's early critics, Desmond MacCarthy identified his mastery of narrative form and his genuine realism as the primary qualities that ensure his success.

Throughout his career Maugham experimented with a wide variety of narrative techniques, conventions, and themes. In his brief introduction to *Orientations*, he classifies his first six stories as experiments, deliberately varied in order that he might discover his literary forte. The early stories mirror the diversity of literary practice one finds in Maugham's early novels. During his first decade as a writer, he produced a naturalistic novel, novels of manners, a Gothic novel, and a historical novel in an effort to discover and develop his gifts as a writer. Although he abandoned some of the techniques of the earliest period, a willingness to experiment marked his later career, for in both short and long fiction his achievements were highly diverse. Yet his most successful stories, and those most likely to last, follow three well-established narrative conventions. In the first the story is narrated from the third-person-omniscient point of view, employing also at times a limited character's point of view. Occasionally a character may represent the author's opinions and attitudes. Prominent examples include "Rain," "The Fall of Edward Barnard," "Red," "The Outstation," "The Letter," and "The Colonel's Lady." In a second type the narrative voice, a thinly veiled version of the author, becomes a participant who meets a character, often in a remote part of the world, and hears his story over dinner or following a game of bridge. Among these, stories like "His Excellency," "Footprints in the Jungle," "The Book Bag," and "A Casual Affair" are Maugham's most successful. In still others the narrator interacts with characters as the plot unfolds over time. Representative titles include "The Alien Corn," "Virtue," "Jane," "The Round Dozen," and "The Voice of the Turtle."

If he was not original in the form of the short story, Maugham must receive credit for the kind of originality he prized and in his own critical writings extolled. From Daisy Griffith to George Peregrine, Maugham has left a galaxy of memorable characters, and since he believed that every living character forms a unique pattern, he can claim originality for those fictional characters he created. Undeniably, they are more memorable than the characters of more distinguished short story writers—Henry James and Katherine Mansfield, for example. Admittedly basing characters on living models, Maugham traveled the world to find their originals, often accompanied by his longtime secretary and companion Gerald Haxton. Their journeys to the South Seas and the Far East opened a rich mine of original characters and themes for Maugham to turn into art. He lived long enough to take satisfaction in his accomplishment, for he pointed out in the preface to the third volume of the Heinemann collected edition that the South Sea stories could not be written again. The advent of airline travel meant that English officials posted to remote parts of the world no longer had to surrender ties to their homeland. They could make regular trips back to England, and thus their characters were less influenced by exotic settings. By the same token, in many stories depicting middle- and upper-class life, he has preserved a way of life in Europe that grew obsolete after World War II.

But Maugham himself may have provided the best explanation of why at least some of his stories are likely to endure. In the introduction to *Tellers of Tales*, one encounters the following observations about authorship: "For what in the long run has the writer to give you? Himself. It is well that he should have breadth of vision, for life in all its extent is his province; but he must not see it only with his own eyes, he must apprehend it with his own nerves, his own heart and his own bowels; his knowledge is partial, of course, but it is distinct, because he is himself and not somebody else. His attitude is definite and characteristic" (*Tellers*, xvii). Maugham correctly extends the concept of a writer's personality to all facets of art, including what the writer sees and is inclined to look for. In large measure the creative artist's contribution derives from a unique character and personality. Yet in the Maugham narrator, one finds the most characteristic expression of his personality. The narrator-persona of Maugham's fiction, from its earliest inception, is the opposite facet of his other alter ego, the emotional and vulnerable Philip Carey from *Of Human Bondage*, for Maugham came to equate emotion with bondage and its control with freedom and maturity. Although critics have sometimes described the detached Maugham persona of the stories as a cynical, less feeling successor to Philip, examination of the early stories demonstrates that his existence precedes Philip's. The very fact that he is a coolheaded observer enhances the reader's emotional involvement with the drama inherent in the story. The pattern of the narrator represents a unique and lasting contribution to fiction, not to be replicated by other narrative voices. The Old Party whom Maugham invited his viewers to equate with Ashenden not only continues to live in Maugham's fiction; he continues to give life to the fiction.

Notes to Part 1

1. Ted Morgan, *Maugham* (New York: Simon & Schuster, 1980), 593.
2. Richard Cordell, *Somerset Maugham: A Biographical and Critical Study* (London: William Heinemann, 1961), 141.
3. *A Writer's Notebook* (London: William Heinemann, 1949), 338; hereafter cited in text as *Notebook*.
4. Garson Kanin, *Remembering Mr. Maugham* (New York: Atheneum, 1966), 255.
5. Morgan, who received this information from Maugham's secretary Alan Searle, raises some doubt as to whether the lost Ashenden stories ever existed (*Maugham*, 206).
6. *Liza of Lambeth* and *On a Chinese Screen* (London: Heron Books, 1967), 323.
7. *Selected Prefaces and Introductions* (New York: Arno Press, 1977), 114.
8. John Pollock, "Somerset Maugham and His Work," *Quarterly Review* 304 (October, 1966): 365–78.
9. *Tellers of Tales* (New York: Doubleday, Doran, 1939), xxvii; hereafter cited in text as *Tellers*.
10. *Points of View* (Garden City, N.Y.: Doubleday, 1959), 176.
11. *The Trembling of a Leaf* (London: Heron Books, 1968), xi.
12. See Raymond Toole-Stott, *A Bibliography of the Works of W. Somerset Maugham* (London: Kaye & Ward, 1973), 200.
13. *Seventeen Lost Stories*, ed. Craig Showalter (Garden City, N.Y.: Doubleday, 1969), 3–4; hereafter cited in text as *Seventeen*.
14. "C'est surtout, par les nouvelles d'un jeune écrivan qu'on peut se rendre compte de son esprit. Il y cherche la voie qui lui est propre dans une série d'essais de genre et de style différents, qui sont comme des orientations, pour trouver son moi littéraire," *Orientations* (London: T. Fisher Unwin, 1899), vi. [It is especially through the short stories of a young writer that one can gather an estimate of his soul. There, in a series of efforts in different styles and types, which are like orientations, he seeks to discover his appropriate voice, his literary self.—Trans.]
15. *Maugham's Choice of Kipling's Best* (Mattituck, N.Y.: Aeonian, 1977), xx.
16. Wilmon Menard, *The Two Worlds of Somerset Maugham* (Los Angeles: Sherbourne Press, 1965), 321.
17. Abe Judson, "Love and Death in the Short Stories of Somerset Maugham: A Psychological Analysis," *Psychiatric Quarterly* 37 (Spring, 1963): 250–62; hereafter cited in text.
18. *The Complete Short Stories of W. Somerset Maugham* (Garden City, N.Y.: Doubleday, 1952), 1:122; hereafter cited in text as *Complete Stories*.
19. *The Casuarina Tree* (New York: Doran, 1926), vi.
20. *Traveller's Library* (Garden City, N.Y.: Doubleday, Doran, 1933), 144.

21. V. S. Pritchett, quoted in *W. Somerset Maugham: The Critical Heritage*, ed. Anthony Curtis and John Whitehead (New York: Routledge & Kegan Paul, 1987), 337.

22. *Ashenden; or, The British Agent* (Garden City, N.Y.: Doubleday, Doran, 1941), 245.

23. Robert Calder, *W. Somerset Maugham and the Quest for Freedom* (Garden City, N.Y.: Doubleday, 1973), 201.

24. *Trio* (Garden City, N.Y.: Doubleday, 1950), 102.

25. John Blackbridge, *The Complete Poker-Player* (New York: Fitzgerald, [1880]). Maugham's only departure in quotations from the original occurs in the following passage: Blackbridge (89) wrote, "In Euchre, which is a contemptible game, the small cards are discarded altogether." Maugham's version reads simply, "Euchre is a contemptible game" (*Complete Stories*, 2:159).

26. In "The Back of Beyond," George Moon paraphrases the aphorism when speaking to Knobby Clark (*Complete Stories*, 1:910).

27. John Whitehead, *Maugham: A Reappraisal* (New York: Barnes & Noble, 1987), 212.

28. W. Somerset Maugham, *The Razor's Edge* (Garden City, N.Y.: Double-day, Doran, Inc., 1944), 1.

29. Joseph Epstein, "Is It All Right to Read Somerset Maugham?" *New Criterion*, 4, No. 3(November, 1985):11.

Part 2

THE WRITER

Introduction

Maugham's writings on the art of the short story are so voluminous that a reader wishing to survey all relevant material would need to examine many volumes. In general he developed his theory of fiction after his most significant stories had been written, but once he began writing criticism, he expounded at great length. Yet he is reasonably consistent and highly repetitive, so that from a few sources one can grasp his essential views.

After *Orientations*, which is introduced by a two-sentence note in French, the separate volumes of short fiction published during Maugham's lifetime include brief prefaces that contribute relevant though minor critical commentary. Often Maugham identifies sources for the items in each volume and makes general observations about the genre. A few of the stories themselves—notably "The Creative Impulse" and "The Human Element"—offer critical perspectives from the narrator that accurately reflect Maugham's views.

Anthologies compiled and edited by Maugham and several nonfiction books incorporate a substantial amount of short story criticism. The introduction to *Tellers of Tales*, an anthology containing 100 stories, provides a long account of the history of the genre and valuable comments on important writers like Chekhov, Maupassant, and Henry James. Two other anthologies, *Traveller's Library* and *W. Somerset Maugham's Introduction to Modern British and American Literature*, include introductions and notes to the sections containing short stories. In *The Summing Up* Maugham provides a lengthy discussion of his narrative art, though in this autobiographical account as elsewhere, he is inclined to deal simultaneously with the novel and the short story. *A Writer's Notebook* reproduces source material from Maugham's journals for stories like "Before the Party," "Rain," and "The Colonel's Lady," as well as scattered notes and comments outlining ideas for stories that were left unwritten.

Maugham's essay "The Short Story," originally a lecture delivered to the British Academy, appeared in *Essays by Divers Hands* and later in *Points of View*. While it repeats much previous material, largely from the introduction to *Tellers of Tales*, it includes a section on Katherine Mansfield's fiction that is useful. Maugham devotes a major portion of the text to biographical accounts of James, Chekhov, and Maupassant. A comment from his introduction to *Tellers of Tales* accounts for his emphasis on biographies of authors in his critiques: "For my part I have always thought that just this, the personality of the creator, was what gave a work of art its lasting interest."[1] In other selections, notably his long introduction to *Kipling's Best* and a short introduction to the works of Dorothy Parker, he writes critical appreciations of the achievements of single authors, again with significant attention to biography. His essay "The Decline and Fall of the Detective Story," published in the 1953 volume *The Vagrant Mood*, praises the detective fiction of Dashiell Hammett and Raymond Chandler.

Among his prefaces the most comprehensive and informative is the preface to *East and West*, the initial volume of his collected short stories. With minor alteration it appeared in the *Saturday Review of Literature* (1934), under the title "How I Write Short Stories." Although it includes lengthy passages on Maupassant and Chekhov, it is the most illuminating account Maugham ever gave of his own art of fiction and for that reason is reproduced here. For the second volume of the collected stories, *The World Over*, Maugham produced a preface largely devoted to practical concerns of the professional writer. Finally, for the three-volume Heinemann collected edition he wrote three separate prefaces. Although exceptionally brief, they include useful information concerning his own literary production.

In the "Notes" on short fiction from *Traveller's Library*, no longer easily accessible, Maugham sets forth his views on a story's form and on the creation of character and offers his evaluations of other writers. Typically, he develops his ideas using comparison and contrast with other literary genres and other arts.

Notes to Introduction

1. W. Somerset Maugham, ed. *Tellers of Tales* (New York: Doubleday, Doran, and Co., Inc., 1939), xxiii.

Preface to *East and West*

This book contains thirty stories. They are all about the same length and on the same scale. The first was written in 1919 and the last in 1931. Though in early youth I had written a number of short stories, for a long time, twelve or fifteen years at least, occupied with the drama, I had ceased to do so; and when a journey to the South Seas unexpectedly provided me with themes that seemed to suit this medium, it was as a beginner of over forty that I wrote the story which is now called *Rain*. Since it caused some little stir the reader of this preface will perhaps have patience with me if I transcribe the working notes, made at the time, on which it was constructed. They are written in hackneyed and slipshod phrases, without grace; for nature has not endowed me with the happy gift of hitting instinctively upon the perfect word to indicate an object and the unusual but apt adjective to describe it. I am travelling from Honolulu to Pago Pago and, hoping they might at some time be of service, I jotted down as usual my impressions of such of my fellow-passengers as attracted my attention. This is what I said of Miss Thompson: "Plump, pretty in a coarse fashion, perhaps not more than twenty-seven. She wore a white dress and a large white hat, long white boots from which the calves bulged in cotton stockings." There had been a raid on the Red Light district in Honolulu just before we sailed and the gossip of the ship spread the report that she was making the journey to escape arrest. My notes go on: "*W. The Missionary*. He was a tall thin man, with long limbs loosely jointed, he had hollow cheeks and high cheek bones, his fine, large, dark eyes were deep in their sockets, he had full sensual lips, he wore his hair rather long. He had a cadaverous air and a look of suppressed fire. His hands were large, with long fingers, rather finely shaped. His naturally pale skin was deeply burned by the tropical sun. *Mrs. W. His Wife*. She was a little woman with her hair very elaborately done, New England; not prominent blue eyes behind gold-rimmed pince-nez, her face was long like a sheep's, but she gave no impression of foolishness, rather of extreme alertness. She had the quick movements of a bird. The most noticeable thing about her was her voice, high, metallic, and without inflection; it fell on the ear with a hard monotony, irritating to the nerves like the ceaseless clamour of a pneumatic drill. She was dressed in black and wore round her neck a gold chain from which hung a small cross. She told me that W. was a missionary on the Gilberts and his district consisting of widely separated islands he frequently had to go distances by canoe. During this time she remained at headquarters and managed the mission. Often the seas were very rough and the journeys were not without peril. He was a medical missionary. She spoke of the depravity of the natives in a voice which nothing could hush, but with a vehement, unctuous horror, telling me of their marriage customs which were obscene beyond description. She said, when first they went it was impossible to find a single good girl in any of the villages. She inveighed against dancing. I talked with the missionary and his wife but once, and with Miss Thompson not at all. Here is the note for the story: "A prostitute, flying from Honolulu after a raid, lands at Pago Pago. There lands there also a missionary and his wife. Also the narrator. All are obliged to stay there owing to an outbreak of measles. The missionary finding out her profession persecutes her. He reduces her to misery, shame, and repentance, he has no mercy on her. He induces the governor to order her return to Honolulu. One morning he is found with his throat cut by his own hand and she is once more radiant and self-possessed. She looks at men and scornfully exclaims: dirty pigs."

An intelligent critic, who combines wide reading and a sensitive taste with a knowledge of the world rare among those who follow his calling, has found in my stories the influence of Guy de Maupassant. That is not strange. When I was a boy he was considered the best short story writer in France and I read his works with avidity. From the age of fifteen whenever I went to Paris I spent most of my afternoons poring over the books in the galleries of the Odéon. I have never passed more enchanted hours. The attendants in their long smocks were indifferent to the people who sauntered about looking at the books and they would let you read for hours without bothering. There was a shelf filled with the works of Guy de Maupassant, but they cost three francs fifty a volume and that was not a sum I was prepared to spend. I had to read as best I could standing up and peering between the uncut pages. Sometimes when no attendant was looking I would hastily cut a page and thus read more conveniently. Fortunately some of them were issued in a cheap edition at seventy-five centimes and I seldom came away without one of these. In this manner, before I was eighteen, I had read all the best stories. It is natural enough that when at that age I began writing stories myself I should unconsciously have chosen those little masterpieces as a model. I might very well have hit upon a worse.

Maupassant's reputation does not stand as high as it did, and it is evident now that there is much in his work to repel. He was a Frenchman of his period in violent reaction against the romantic age which was finishing in the saccharine sentimentality of Octave Feuillet (admired by Matthew Arnold) and in the impetuous slop of George Sand. He was a naturalist, aiming at truth at all costs, but the truth he achieved looks to us now a trifle superficial. He does not analyse his characters. He takes little interest in the reason why. They act, but wherefore he does not know. "For me," he says, "psychology in a novel or in a story consists in this: to show the inner man by his life." That is very well, that is what we all try to do, but the gesture will not by itself always indicate the motive. The result with Maupassant was a simplification of character which is effective enough in a short story, but on reflection leaves you unconvinced. There is more in men than that, you say. Again, he was obsessed by the tiresome notion, common then to his countrymen, that it was a duty a man owed himself to hop into bed with every woman under forty that he met. His characters indulge their sexual desire to gratify their self-esteem. They are like the people who eat caviare when they are not hungry because it is expensive. Perhaps the only human emotion that affects his characters with passion is avarice. This he can understand; it fills him with horror, but notwithstanding he has a sneaking sympathy with it. He was slightly common. But for all this it would be foolish to deny his excellence. An author has the right to be judged by his best work. No author is perfect. You must accept his defects; they are often the necessary complement of his merits; and this may be said in gratitude to posterity that it is very willing to do this. It takes what is good in a writer and is not troubled by what is bad. It goes so far sometimes, to the confusion of the candid reader, as to claim a profound significance for obvious faults. So you will see the critics (the awe-inspiring voice of posterity) find subtle reasons to explain to his credit something in a play of Shakespeare's that any dramatist could tell them needed no other explanation than haste, indifference or wilfulness. Maupassant's stories are good stories. The anecdote is interesting apart from the narration so that it would secure attention if it were told over the dinner-table; and that seems to me a very great merit indeed. However halting your words and insipid your rendering, you could not fail to interest your listeners if you told them the bare story of *Boule de Suif*, *L'Héritage* or *La Parure*. These stories have a beginning, a middle and an end. They do not wander along an uncertain line so that you cannot see whither they are leading, but follow without hesitation, from exposition to climax, a bold and vigorous curve. It may be that they have no great spiritual significance. Maupassant did not aim at that. He looked upon himself as a plain man; no good writer was ever less a man of letters. He did not pretend to be a philosopher, and here he was well-advised, for when he indulges in reflection he is commonplace. But within his limits he is admirable. He has an astonishing capacity for creating living people. He can afford little space, but in a few pages can set before you half a dozen persons so sharply seen and vividly described that you know all about them that you need. Their outline is clear; they are distinguishable from one another; and they breathe the breath of life. They have no complexity, they lack strangely the indecision, the unexpectedness, the mystery that we see in human beings; they are in fact simplified for the purposes of the story. But they are not deliberately simplified: those keen eyes of his saw clearly, but they did not see profoundly; it is a happy chance that they saw all that was necessary for him to achieve the aim he had in view. He treats the surroundings in the same way, he sets his scene accurately, briefly and effectively; but whether he is describing the charming landscape of Normandy or the stuffy, overcrowded drawing-rooms of the eighties his object is the same, to get on with the story. On his own lines I do not think that Maupassant is likely to be surpassed. If his excellence is not at the moment so apparent it is because what he wrote must now stand comparison with the very different, more subtle and moving work of Chekov.

No one's stock to-day stands higher with the best critics than Chekov's. In fact he has put every other story-teller's nose out of joint. To admire him is a proof of good taste; not to like him is to declare yourself a philistine. His stories are the models that young writers naturally take. This is understandable. On the face of it it is easier to write stories like Chekov's than stories like Maupassant's. To invent a story interesting in itself apart from the telling is a difficult thing, the power to do it is a gift of nature, it cannot be acquired by taking thought, and it is a gift that very few people have. Chekov had many gifts, but not this one. If you try to tell one of his stories you will find that there is nothing to tell. The anecdote, stripped of its trimmings, is insignificant and often inane. It was grand for people who wanted to write a story and couldn't think of a plot to discover that you could very well manage without one. If you could take two or three persons, describe their mutual relations and leave it at that, why then it wasn't so hard to write a story; and if you could flatter yourself that this really was art, what could be more charming?

But I am not quite sure that it is wise to found a technique on a writer's defects. I have little doubt that Chekov would have written stories with an ingenious, original and striking plot if he had been able to think of them. It was not in his temperament. Like all good writers he made a merit of his limitations. Was it not Goethe who said that an artist only achieves greatness when he recognises them? If a short story is a piece of prose dealing with more or less imaginary persons no one wrote better short stories than Chekov. If, however, as some think, it should be the representation of an action, complete in itself and of a certain limited length, he leaves something to be desired. He put his own idea clearly enough in these words: "Why write about a man getting into a submarine and going to the North Pole to reconcile himself to the world, while his beloved at that moment throws herself with a hysterical shriek from the belfry? All this is untrue and does not happen in real life. One must write about simple things: how Peter Semionovitch married Maria Ivanovna. That is all." But there is no reason why a writer should not make a story of an unusual incident. The fact that something happens every day does not make it more important. The pleasure of recognition, which is the pleasure thus aimed at, is the lowest of the aesthetic pleasures. It is not a merit in a story that it is undramatic. Maupassant chose very ordinary people and sought to show what there was of drama in the common happenings of their lives. He chose the significant incident and extracted from it all the drama possible. It is a method as praiseworthy as another; it tends to make a story more absorbing. Probability is not the only test; and probability is a constantly changing thing. At one time it was accepted that the "call of the blood" should enable long-lost children to recognize their parents and that a woman only had to get into men's clothes to pass as a man. Probability is what you can get the readers of your time to swallow. Nor did Chekov, notwithstanding his principles, adhere to his canon unless it suited him. Take one of the most beautiful and touching of his stories, *The Bishop*. It describes the approach of death with great tenderness, but there is no reason for the Bishop to die, and a better technician would have made the cause of death an integral part of the story. "Everything that has no relation to the story must be ruthlessly thrown away," he says in his advice to Schoukin. "If in the first chapter you say that a gun hung on the wall in the second or third chapter it must without fail be discharged." So when the Bishop eats some tainted fish and a few days later dies of typhoid we may suppose that it was the tainted fish that killed him. If that is so he did not die of typhoid, but of ptomaine poisoning, and the symptoms were not as described. But of course Chekov did not care. He was determined that his good and gentle bishop should die and for his own purposes he wanted him to die in a particular way. I do not understand the people who say of Chekov's stories that they are slices of life, I do not understand, that is, if they mean that they offer a true and typical picture of life. I do not believe they do that, nor do I believe they ever did. I think they are marvellously lifelike, owing to the writer's peculiar talent, but I think they are deliberately chosen to square with the prepossessions of a sick, sad and overworked, gray-minded man. I do not blame them for that. Every writer sees the world in his own way and gives you his own picture of it. The imitation of life is not a reasonable aim of art; it is a discipline to which the artist from time to time subjects himself when the stylization of life has reached an extravagance that outrages common sense. For Chekov life is like a game of billiards in which you never pot the red, bring off a losing hazard or make a cannon, and should you by a miraculous chance get a fluke you will almost certainly cut the cloth. He sighs sadly because the futile do not succeed, the idle do not work, liars do not speak the truth, drunkards are not sober and the ignorant have no culture. I suppose that it is this attitude that makes his chief characters somewhat indistinct. He can give you a striking portrait of a man in two lines, as much as can be said of anyone in two lines to set before you a living person, but with elaboration he seems to lose his grasp of the individual. His men are shadowy creatures, with vague impulses to good, but without will-power, shiftless, untruthful, fond of fine words, often with great ideals, but with no power of action. His women are lachrymose, slatternly and feeble-minded. Though they think it a sin they will commit fornication with anyone who asks them, not because they have passion, not even because they want to, but because it is too much trouble to refuse. It is only in his description of young girls that he seems touched with a tender indulgence. "Alas! regardless of their doom, the little victims play." He is moved by their charm, the gaiety of their laughter, their ingenuousness and their vitality; but it all leads to nothing. They make no effort to conquer their happiness, but yield passively to the first obstacle in the way.

But if I have ventured to make these observations I beg the reader not to think that I have anything but a very great admiration for Chekov. No writer, I repeat, is faultless. It is well to admire him for his merits. Not to recognize his imperfections, but rather to insist that they are excellencies, can in the long run only hurt his reputation. Chekov is extremely readable. That is a writer's supreme virtue and one upon which sufficient stress is often not laid. He shared it with Maupassant. Both of them were professional writers who turned out stories at more or less regular intervals to earn their living. They wrote as a doctor visits his patients or a solicitor sees his clients. It was part of the day's work. They had to please their readers. They were not always inspired, it was only now and then that they produced a masterpiece, but it is very seldom that they wrote anything that did not hold the reader's attention to the last line. They both wrote for papers and magazines. Sometimes a critic will describe a book of short stories as magazine stories and thus in his own mind damn them. That is foolish. No form of art is produced unless there is a demand for it and if newspapers and magazines did not publish short stories they would not be written. All stories are magazine stories or newspaper stories. The writers must accept certain (but constantly changing) conditions; it has never been known yet that a good writer was unable to write his best owing to the conditions under which alone he could gain a public for his work. That has never been anything but an excuse of the second-rate. I suspect that Chekov's great merit of concision is due to the fact that the newspapers for which he habitually wrote could only give him a certain amount of space. He said that stories should have neither a beginning nor an end. He could not have meant that literally. You might as well ask of a fish that it should have neither head nor tail. It would not be a fish if it hadn't. The way Chekov in reality begins a story is wonderfully good. He gives the facts at once, in a few lines; he has an unerring feeling for the essential statements, and he sets them down baldly, but with great precision, so that you know at once whom you have to deal with and what the circumstances are. Maupassant often started his stories with an introduction designed to put the reader in a certain frame of mind. It is a dangerous method only justified by success. It may be dull. It may throw the reader off the scent; you have won his interest in certain characters and then instead of being told what you would like to know about them, your interest is claimed for other people in other circumstances. Chekov preached compactness. In his longer stories he did not always achieve it. He was distressed by the charge brought against him that he was indifferent to moral and sociological questions and when he had ample space at his command he seized the opportunity to show that they meant as much to him as to any other right-thinking person. Then in long and somewhat tedious conversations he would make his characters express his own conviction that, whatever the conditions of things might be then, at some not far distant date (say 1934) the Russians would be free, tyranny would exist no longer, the poor would hunger no more and happiness, peace and brotherly love rule in the vast empire. But these were aberrations forced upon him by the pressure of opinion (common in all countries) that the writer of fiction should be a prophet, a social reformer and a philosopher. In his shorter stories Chekov attained the concision he aimed at in a manner that is almost miraculous.

And no one had a greater gift than he for giving you the intimate feeling of a place, a landscape, a conversation or (within his limited range) a character. I suppose this is what people mean by the vague word atmosphere. Chekov seems to have achieved it very simply, without elaborate explanation or long description, by a precise narration of facts; and I think it was due with him to a power of seeing things with amazing naïvety. The Russians are a semi-barbarous people and they seem to have retained the power of seeing things naturally, as though they existed in a vacuum; while we in the West, with our complicated culture behind us, see things with the associations they have gathered during long centuries of civilization. They almost seem to see the thing in itself. Most writers, especially those living abroad, have in the last few years been shown numbers of stories by Russian refugees who vainly hope to earn a few guineas by placing them somewhere. Though dealing with the present day they might very well be stories by Chekov not at his best; they all have that direct, sincere vision. It is a national gift. In no one was it more acutely developed than in Chekov.

But I have not yet pointed out what to my mind is Chekov's greatest merit. Since I am not a critic and do not know the proper critical expressions I am obliged to describe this as best I can in terms of my own feeling. Chekov had an amazing power of surrounding people with air so that, though he does not put them before you in the round and they lack the coarse, often brutal vitality of Maupassant's figures, they live with a strange and unearthly life. They are not lit by the hard light of common day but suffused in a mysterious grayness. They move in this as though they were disembodied spirits. It is their souls that you seem to see. The subconscious seems to come to the surface and they communicate with one another directly without the impediment of speech. Strange, futile creatures, with descriptions of their outward seeming tacked on them like a card on an exhibit in a museum, they move as mysteriously as the tortured souls who crowded about Dante when he walked in Hell. You have the feeling of a vast, gray, lost throng wandering aimless in some dim underworld. It fills you with awe and with uneasiness. I have hinted that Chekov had no great talent for inventing a multiplicity of persons. Under different names, with different environment, the same characters recur. It is as though, when you look at the soul, the superficial difference vanishes and everyone is more or less the same. His people seem strangely to slip into one another as though they were not distinct individuals, but temporary fictions, and as though in truth they were all part of one another. The importance of a writer in the long run rests on his uniqueness. I do not know that anyone but Chekov has so poignantly been able to represent spirit communing with spirit. It is this that makes one feel that Maupassant in comparison is obvious and vulgar. The strange, the terrible thing is that, looking at man in their different ways, these two great writers, Maupassant and Chekov, saw eye to eye. One was content to look upon the flesh, the other, more nobly and subtly, surveyed the spirit; but they agreed that life was tedious and insignificant and that men were base, unintelligent and pitiful.

I hope the reader will not be impatient with me because in an introduction to my own stories I have dwelt at length on these remarkable writers. Maupassant and Chekov are the two authors of short stories whose influence survives to the present day and all of us who cultivate the medium must in the end be judged by the standards they have set.

So far as I could remember it I have placed the stories in this volume in the order in which they were written. I thought it might possibly interest the reader to see how I had progressed from the tentativeness of the first ones, when I was very much at the mercy of my anecdote, to the relative certainty of the later ones when I had learnt so to arrange my material as to attain the result I wanted. Though all but two have been published in a magazine these stories were not written with that end in view. When I began to write them I was fortunately in a position of decent independence and I wrote them as a relief from work which I thought I had been too long concerned with. It is often said that stories are no better than they are because the editors of magazines insist on their being written to a certain pattern. This has not been my experience. All but *Rain* and *The Book-Bag* were published in the *Cosmopolitan* magazine and Ray Long, the Editor, never put pressure on me to write other than as I wished. Sometimes the stories were cut and this is reasonable since no editor can afford one contributor more than a certain amount of space; but I was never asked to make the smallest alteration to suit what might be supposed to be the taste of the readers. Ray Long paid me for them not only with good money, but with generous appreciation. I did not value this less. We authors are simple, childish creatures and we treasure a word of praise from those who buy our wares. Most of them were written in groups from notes made as they occurred to me, and in each group I left naturally enough to the last those that seemed most difficult to write. A story is difficult to write when you do not know *all* about it from the beginning, but for part of it must trust to your imagination and experience. Sometimes the curve does not intuitively present itself and you have to resort to this method and that to get the appropriate line.

I beg the reader not to be deceived by the fact that a good many of these stories are told in the first person into thinking that they are experiences of my own. This is merely a device to gain verisimilitude. It is one that has its defects, for it may strike the reader that the narrator could not know all the events he sets forth; and when he tells a story in the first person at one remove, when he reports, I mean, a story that someone tells him, it may very well seem that the speaker, a police officer, for example, or a sea-captain, could never have expressed himself with such facility and with such elaboration. Every convention has its disadvantages. These must be as far as possible disguised and what cannot be disguised must be accepted. The advantage of this one is its directness. It makes it possible for the writer to tell no more than he knows. Making no claim to omniscience, he can frankly say when a motive or an occurrence is unknown to him, and thus often give his story a plausibility that it might otherwise lack. It tends also to put the reader on intimate terms with the author. Since Maupassant and Chekov, who tried so hard to be objective, nevertheless are so nakedly personal, it has sometimes seemed to me that if the author can in no way keep himself out of his work it might be better if he put in as much of himself as possible. The danger is that he may put in too much and thus be as boring as a talker who insists on monopolizing the conversation. Like all conventions this one must be used with discretion. The reader may have observed that in the original note of *Rain* the narrator was introduced, but in the story as written omitted.

Three of the stories in this volume were told me and I had nothing to do but make them probable, coherent and dramatic. They are *The Letter*, *Footprints in the Jungle* and *The Book-Bag*. The rest were invented, as I have shown *Rain* was, by the accident of my happening upon persons here and there, who in themselves or from something I heard about them suggested a theme that seemed suitable for a short story. This brings me to a topic that has always concerned writers and that has at times given the public, the writer's raw material, some uneasiness. There are authors who state that they never have a living model in mind when they create a character. I think they are mistaken. They are of this opinion because they have not scrutinized with sufficient care the recollections and impressions upon which they have constructed the person who, they fondly imagine, is of their invention. If they did they would discover that, unless he was taken from some book they had read, a practise by no means uncommon, he was suggested by one or more persons they had at one time known or seen. The great writers of the past made no secret of the fact that their characters were founded on living people. We know that the good Sir Walter Scott, a man of the highest principles, portrayed his father, with sharpness first and then, when the passage of years had changed his temper, with tolerance; Henri Beyle, in the manuscript of at least one of his novels, has written in at the side of the real persons who were his models; and this is what Turgenev himself says: "For my part, I ought to confess that I never attempted to create a type without having, not an idea, but a living person, in whom the various elements were harmonized together, to work from. I have always needed some groundwork on which I could tread firmly." With Flaubert it is the same story; that Dickens used his friends and relations freely is notorious; and if you read the Journal of Jules Renard, a most instructive book to anyone who wishes to know how a writer works, you will see the care with which he set down every little detail about the habits, ways of speech and appearance of the persons he knew. When he came to write a novel he made use of this storehouse of carefully collected information. In Chekov's diary you will find notes which were obviously made for use at some future time, and in the recollections of his friends there are frequent references to the persons who were the originals of certain of his characters. It looks as though the practice were very common. I should have said it was necessary and inevitable. Its convenience is obvious. You are much more likely to depict a character who is a recognizable human being, with his own individuality, if you have a living model. The imagination can create nothing out of the void. It needs the stimulus of sensation. The writer whose creative faculty has been moved by something peculiar in a person (peculiar perhaps only to the writer) falsifies his idea if he attempts to describe that person other than as he sees him. Character hangs together and if you try to throw people off the scent, by making a short man tall for example (as though stature had no effect on character) or by making him choleric when he has the concomitant traits of an equable temper, you will destroy the plausible harmony (to use the beautiful phrase of Baltasar Gracian) of which it consists. The whole affair would be plain sailing if it were not for the feelings of the persons concerned. The writer has to consider the vanity of the human race and the Schadenfreude which is one of its commonest and most detestable failings. A man's friends will find pleasure in recognizing him in a book and though the author may never even have seen him will point out to him, especially if it is unflattering, what they consider his living image. Often someone will recognize a trait he knows in himself or a description of the place he lives in and in his conceit jumps to the conclusion that the character described is a portrait of himself. Thus in the story called *The Outstation* the Resident was suggested by a British Consul I had once known in Spain and it was written ten years after his death, but I have heard that the Resident of a district in Sarawak, which I described in the story, was much affronted because he thought I had had him in mind. The two men had not a trait in common. I do not suppose any writer attempts to draw an exact portrait. Nothing, indeed, is so unwise as to put into a work of fiction a person drawn line by line from life. His values are all wrong, and, strangely enough, he does not make the other characters in the story seem false, but himself. He never convinces. That is why the many writers who have been attracted by the singular and powerful figure of the late Lord Northcliffe have never succeeded in presenting a credible personage. The model a writer chooses is seen through his own temperament and if he is a writer of any originality what he sees need have little relation with the facts. He may see a tall man short or a generous one avaricious; but, I repeat, if he sees him tall, tall he must remain. He takes only what he wants of the living man. He uses him as a peg on which to hang his own fancies. To achieve his end (the plausible harmony that nature so seldom provides) he gives him traits that the model does not possess. He makes him coherent and substantial. The created character, the result of imagination founded on fact, is art, and life in the raw, as we know, is of this only the material. The odd thing is that when the charge is made that an author has copied this person or the other from life, emphasis is laid only on his less praiseworthy characteristics. If you say of a character that he is kind to his mother, but beats his wife, everyone will cry: Ah, that's Brown, how beastly to say he beats his wife; and no one thinks for a moment of Jones and Robinson who are notoriously kind to their mothers. I draw from this the somewhat surprising conclusion that we know our friends by their vices and not by their virtues. I have stated that I never even spoke to Miss Thompson in *Rain*. This is a character that the world has not found wanting in vividness. Though but one of a multitude of writers my practise is doubtless common to most, so that I may be permitted to give another instance of it. I was once asked to meet at dinner two persons, a husband and wife, of whom I was told only what the reader will shortly read. I think I never knew their names. I should certainly not recognize them if I met them in the street. Here are the notes I made at the time. "A stout, rather pompous man of fifty, with pince-nez, gray-haired, a florid complexion, blue eyes, a neat gray moustache. He talks with assurance. He is resident of an outlying district and is somewhat impressed with the importance of his position. He despises the men who have let themselves go under influence of the climate and the surroundings. He has travelled extensively during his short leaves in the East and knows Java, the Philippines, the coast of China and the Malay Peninsula. He is very British, very patriotic; he takes a great deal of exercise. He has been a very heavy drinker and always took a bottle of whiskey to bed with him. His wife has entirely cured him and now he drinks nothing but water. She is a little insignificant woman, with sharp features, thin, with a sallow skin and a flat chest. She is very badly dressed. She has all the prejudices of an Englishwoman. All her family for generations have been in second-rate regiments. Except that you know that she has caused her husband to cease drinking entirely you would think her quite colourless and unimportant." On these materials I invented the story which is called *Before the Party*. I do not believe that any candid person could think that these two people had cause for complaint because they had been made use of. It is true that I should never have thought of the story if I had not met them, but anyone who takes the trouble to read it will see how insignificant was the incident (the taking of the bottle to bed) that suggested it and how differently the two chief characters have in the course of writing developed from the brief sketch which was their foundation.

"Critics are like horse-flies which prevent the horse from ploughing," said Chekov. "For over twenty years I have read criticisms of my stories, and I do not remember a single remark of any value or one word of valuable advice. Only once Skabichevsky wrote something which made an impression on me. He said I would die in a ditch, drunk." He was writing for twenty-five years and during that time his writing was constantly attacked. I do not know whether the critics of the present day are naturally of a less ferocious temper; I must allow that on the whole the judgment that has been passed on the stories in this volume when from time to time a collection has been published in book form has been favourable. One epithet, however, has been much applied to them, which has puzzled me; they have been described with disconcerting frequency as "competent." Now on the face of it I might have thought this laudatory, for to do a thing competently is certainly more deserving of praise than to do it incompetently, but the adjective has been used in a disparaging sense and, anxious to learn and if possible to improve, I have asked myself what was in the mind of the critics who thus employed it. Of course none of us is liked by everybody and it is necessary that a man's writing, which is so intimate a revelation of himself, should be repulsive to persons who are naturally antagonistic to the creature he is. This should leave him unperturbed. But when an author's work is somewhat commonly found to have a quality that is unattractive to many it is sensible to him to give the matter his attention. There is evidently something that a number of people do not like in my stories and it is this they try to express when they damn them with the faint praise of competence. I have a notion that it is the definiteness of their form. I hazard the suggestion (perhaps unduly flattering to myself) because this particular criticism has never been made in France where my stories have had with the critics and the public much greater success than they have had in England. The French, with their classical sense and their orderly minds, demand a precise form and are exasperated by a work in which the ends are left lying about, themes are propounded and not resolved and a climax is foreseen and then eluded. This precision on the other hand has always been slightly antipathetic to the English. Our great novels have been shapeless and this, far from disconcerting their readers, has given them a sense of security. This is the life we know, they have thought, with its arbitrariness and inconsequence; we can put out of our minds the irritating thought that two and two make four. If I am right in this surmise I can do nothing about it and I must resign myself to being called competent for the rest of my days. My prepossessions in the arts are on the side of law and order. I like a story that fits. I did not take to writing stories seriously till I had had much experience as a dramatist, and this experience taught me to leave out everything that did not serve the dramatic value of my story. It taught me to make incident follow incident in such a manner as to lead up to the climax I had in mind. I am not unaware of the disadvantages of this method. It gives a tightness of effect that is sometimes disconcerting. You feel that life does not dovetail into its various parts with such neatness. In life stories straggle, they begin nowhere and tail off without a point. That is probably what

Chekov meant when he said that stories should have neither a beginning nor an end. It is certain that sometimes it gives you a sensation of airlessness when you see persons who behave so exactly according to character, and incidents that fall into place with such perfect convenience. The story-teller of this kind aims not only at giving his own feelings about life, but at a formal decoration. He arranges life to suit his purposes. He follows a design in his mind, leaving out this and changing that; he distorts facts to his advantage, according to his plan; and when he attains his object produces a work of art. It may be that life slips through his fingers; then he has failed; it may be that he seems sometimes so artificial that you cannot believe him, and when you do not believe a story-teller he is done. When he succeeds he has given you the pleasure of following out the pattern he has drawn on the surface of chaos. But he seeks to prove nothing. He paints a picture and sets it before you. You can take it or leave it.

Notes on the Short Story
from *Traveller's Library*

I wish I knew some book on the art and theory of the short story, so that I could read it and give the reader an authoritative view on the question; I do not, and so must content myself with offering him my own reflections. I do not set them down with confidence. I have written a good many short stories myself, but no writer writes what he wants to, he writes what he can, and it is natural enough that he should think the best way to do a thing is the way he does it. One would like to make up one's mind exactly what a short story is. One would like to be certain how it differs from the novel. Of course you can say that a short story is a piece of fiction of not more than so many pages and a novel is a piece of fiction of not so many more. That is easy. It would be difficult to fix the number. The French now seem to write novels that are shorter and shorter. What are you to say of François Mauriac, perhaps the most interesting of the younger French novelists, who describes as a novel a book of two hundred pages of large print? It is shorter than many a piece of fiction that its author has published as a short story. I suggest first of all that length has nothing to do with the case. There is no reason why you should not have a novel in five pages and a short story in three hundred. I think the short story is something very different from the novel, but it is a difference that many celebrated authors have not realised; or if they have, it may be that they have not cared. For example take a celebrated story by Chekov called *The Lady with the Dog*. Well, to my mind that is not a short story, but a short novel: on the other hand the same author's *Peasants*, which is about as long, very well fulfills the demands I make of a short story. Some writers write short stories of the length of a novel, and there may not be a word too much in them; but they remain short stories. The best example I know of this is Frank Swinnerton's *Nocturne*.

It may be that the element of time is important. I am never comfort-

By permission of A. P. Watt Limited on behalf of the Royal Literary Trust and William Heinemann Limited.

ably at home with a short story the action of which takes place during many months or years. The passing of time and the changes it effects have been much studied in fiction of late, and the subject is fascinating, especially now that we have become as perhaps never before conscious of change, but it does not seem proper to the short story. I think it possible that the short story should occupy itself with a single moment of time. I was interested to see how Aldous Huxley, than whom no writer is more aware of what he is about, in a story called *Chawdron*, in which he related events that had occurred during many years, used the device of making the narrator tell the story to a friend in the interval between breakfast and luncheon. In this ingenious way he used the materials of a novel for a very well constructed short story. There is something static in the short story; the novel is dynamic. In the latter one thing leads to another; in the former it stays put. One of the most interesting things in modern fiction has been the discovery that it is possible to show the change in personality that the events of life occasion. It is because there is nothing of this in the older novels that they seem to us so unreal. Take *La Cousine Bette*, for instance, one of the best novels, by, take it all in all, the greatest novelist that ever lived. You are told all about Madame Marneffe the first time she is described, she is given you in all her horror, and she remains throughout what she was at the beginning. She neither changes nor developes. Then there is Harold Skimpole. A full length portrait of him is drawn on his first appearance and the reader knows no more about him at the end of a long book than he knew then. Dickens had told all he knew at once and there was nothing more to add. It is on this account perhaps that these novelists were driven to melodramatic incident. When the characters are frozen (like German credits) the story is the only way in which the author can hold his reader's attention. The short story does not aim at the developement of character; nor does it aim at the discovery of character. I mean by this the process by which an author presents you with an enigmatic creature whose personality is gradually divulged; he confronts you with a mystery and its solution may have all the excitement of a detective story. The short-story writer can only show what his people are at the moment he chooses to interfere in their fates. He has no space to show any change in them and no time to be secret about them. So far as he uses incident to portray character his intrigue must be simple. If, however, he is not interested in character, but only in the story, I do not see why this should not be as complicated as he likes. You have a very good example of this in *The Second-Class Passenger* by Perceval Gibbons. The shortness of time occupied by the events related gives the author the unity necessary to the form. I seem forced by what I have said to the following definition: the short story is a piece of fiction, of any length you choose, which deals with a single situation, but this situation may be a mood, a character or an event. It is only the fashion of the moment that decrees that the delineation of a mood is of more consequence than the other two. Indeed, looking back on the past, it is possible to argue that the narration of an event has more chance of enduring than the description of a mood or the analysis of a character. But they say that example is better than precept and so I point to the following stories as, in their several ways, excellent specimens of the form.

Notes on the Short Story
from *Traveller's Library*

In the earlier section of this book which I devoted to short stories I printed the works of some of the older writers. I think they had a pleasing variety. I should like to call the reader's attention particularly to Arthur Machen's *The Inmost Light*, because he is an author too little known who writes this language of ours with great beauty. I have myself a weakness for the short story that has a precise form. I like it to have a beginning, a middle and an end. I do not want to be left in doubt about what happens. I like the author to say everything to the point that he has to say on the subject of his choice. That is the old-fashioned method. It is the one practised by that great master of the short story Guy de Maupassant. It is the one practised by Mr. Rudyard Kipling in the beautiful story *Without Benefit of Clergy* which I wish I could have persuaded him to allow me to print. But I am aware that the method gives a certain tightness of effect which is sometimes disconcerting. You feel that life does not dovetail into its various parts with such neatness. In life stories straggle, they begin nowhere and tail off without a point. It gives you a sensation of airlessness when you see persons who behave so exactly according to character and incidents that fit the frame with such perfect convenience. You have just the same feeling as when you look at one of those great landscapes of the seventeenth century in which the composition has such an architectural balance, the mass of a tree corresponding with the mass of a cloud, the light and shade forming a definite pattern, and compare it with the haphazard arrangements of nature. The reason is obvious. These painters used nature as an excuse for a formal decoration. They were not interested in its fleeting beauty but in its stately grandeur. Their intention was not to portray landscape, but to create a work of art. Life for the most part escaped them; they did not care, they achieved what they aimed at. So it was also with the story writers of the older school. They arranged life to suit their purposes. They followed the patterns in their minds, they left out this and changed that, distorting facts to their advantage, according to their design; and when they attained their object produced a work of art. But in their case too life often fell by the way. Sometimes they seemed so artificial that you could not believe them, and when you do not believe a story-teller he is done. Sometimes the elegance of the design was intolerable. It is not surprising that there was a reaction. To the best of my belief it came from Russia. The great Russian writers (with the possible exception of Turgeniev) have had a very inadequate sense of form. I have a notion that most of the revolutionary changes in the arts have taken place owing to the inability of an artist, or a group of artists, to conform to the usages of his time. He has been forced to originality because he could not express himself in current terms. Cézanne tried his best to paint like Delacroix and it was only because he couldn't that he learned gradually to paint in a way that has revolutionised the whole of modern painting. I think it was because the Russians could not write the neat, rounded, well-constructed stories that the French wrote with such mastery that they developed the new technique that has had so much influence on the short-story writers of the present day. You see the beginnings of the new method in Tolstoi, but it was Chekov who brought it to perfection. It is hard to begin a story without a beginning and Chekov begins his no differently from Guy de Maupassant. But here the resemblance ends. Incidents are told you that lead to nothing. As often as not there is no climax. Often they tail off, leaving you in the air. Sometimes they remind you of a man who thought he could build a house by laying a thousand bricks alongside of one another. You are then given the materials for a story and asked to construct it yourself. Sometimes the stories consist merely of an incident thrown at you without rhyme or reason. Sometimes they are merely the description of a character in a void. Sometimes they are no more than the noting down of a passing mood. Of course, thus liberated from the restraints of a rigid form, verisimilitude is admirably attained. This is life, you say, with its loose ends, it arbitrariness, its inconsequence. These stories seem indeed wide open to the winds of heaven; they can make the others, with their careful arrangements, their points so skilfully worked up to, seem outrageously stilted. But just as the stories of the old kind run the danger of artificiality, so these run the danger of inanity. Chekov himself did not always escape it. His followers less often still. For, as I said just now, he has had a great influence on the writers of short stories. In England especially we have never taken so keen an interest in form as the orderly and logical French. Witness the shapeless novels of the great novelists from Richardson down to the late Victorians. And the method was deceptively easy. Why, if it was merely a question of going to a hairdresser's to get shaved, and you only had to describe the process and when the barber after cutting your chin confided in you that his girl had gone to the pictures the night before with the milkman, then anyone could write a short story. But there was a little more in it than that. The loose construction of a story by Chekov gave the imagination room to play, the vagueness had its own significance and all that was left out demanded from the reader an active and pleasant collaboration. But no reader gets out of a novel or a short story more than the author has put in. The reader gets so much out of Chekov's best stories because he put a great deal in.

Probably of all the modern writers who have been influenced by Chekov Katherine Mansfield is the best. I admire her delicate insight, her minute appreciation of the appearance of things and her lucid and easy English, but I cannot think that she has used the manner in her longer stories with complete success. I feel in them the want of a supporting skeleton. They remind me of jelly-fishes, iridescent and strangely lovely as they float aimlessly about the sea, but floppy and inert. I like them page by page, but I do not quite know what they are all about, and I finish them with a slight sense of having been taken in. Her shorter stories on the other hand seem to me to have great excellence. They can do without a backbone. In them her charming gifts are admirably shown. The reader will find the same method employed in other stories in this section and employed to my mind with uncommon felicity. I end with two compositions by Mr. Harold Nicholson. I very much wanted to insert them, but did not quite know how I should describe them. They are not exactly essays, and if they are short stories they are short stories in a new manner; they purport to be reminiscences, but so do many short stories; they have the art and grace of fiction and they are written in a conversational and urbane style that is very well suited to fiction. If fiction is life rearranged for the purpose of pleasure then they are very distinctly fiction. They seem to me entirely delightful and I should have been very glad to include in this book the whole volume from which I have been fortunately allowed to choose two pieces.

Part 3

THE CRITICS

Introduction

After the lapse of more than a decade following the appearance of *Orientations*, Maugham published his next story at age 46. By that time he was a world-famous novelist and dramatist, and as a result his subsequent short story collections were assured of widespread attention by reviewers, among them eminent critics. A representative selection of contemporary reviews can be found in Curtis and Whitehead's *W. Somerset Maugham: The Critical Heritage*. Scholarly journals, however, were less hospitable to articles than other periodicals, and those on Maugham's stories, even today, are few. Among them the most comprehensive and informative is Abe Judson's "Love and Death in the Short Stories of W. Somerset Maugham: A Psychological Analysis," which follows a statistical methodology in its exploration of Maugham's themes and character types.

Most book-length surveys of Maugham's work include one or more chapters on the short fiction; collectively, they offer a richly diverse source of critical perspectives and evaluations. Books by Richard Cordell, Robert Calder, Anthony Curtis, Forrest Burt, John Whitehead, and Archie Loss remain the most accessible and illuminating critical sources for the student of Maugham.

The selections that follow are intended as a representative cross-section of Maugham criticism, including negative as well as favorable views. In his review of *East and West*, Graham Greene devotes attention to Maugham's critical canons. H. E. Bates attempts to place Maugham within the context of the development of short fiction, though Bates, himself an accomplished artist in the genre, weighs heavily Maugham's potential as a model for other writers. In his introduction to an anthology of Maugham stories, Angus Wilson assesses Maugham's merits in order to explain his selection of 12 stories for publication. Archie Loss's "White Magic" forms an entire chapter in his critical introduction to Maugham's work. By centering on a few titles, Loss achieves sound critical insight within a limited space.

Graham Greene

Mr. Somerset Maugham's tales are so well known to all who are interested in the art of the short story that a reviewer may be forgiven for dwelling chiefly on the preface Mr. Maugham has contributed to this beautifully produced volume. It is a finely written, delightfully "sensible" essay on the short story, and it is the more valuable because it represents a point of view not common to many English writers. Mr. Maugham represents Maupassant's influence when most English short-story writers of any merit represent Chekov's.

Mr. Maugham can write nothing without inspiring confidence; he is a writer of great deliberation even when his style is most careless ("burning mouth," "nakedness of soul," "mouth like a scarlet wound"); he will never, one feels, lose his head; he has a steady point of view. The banality of the phrases I have noted do not indicate an emotional abandonment; they indicate a rather blasé attitude towards the details of his stories; narrative is something which has to be got through before the point of his anecdote appears, and Mr. Maugham is sometimes a little bored and off-hand in the process. The anecdote to Mr. Maugham is very nearly everything; the anecdote, and not the characters, not the "atmosphere," not the style, is primarily responsible for conveying Mr. Maugham's attitude; and it is anecdote as contrasted with spiritual analysis: Maupassant with Chekov: that he discusses in his preface with great justice to the opposite school.

> I do not know that anyone but Chekov has so poignantly been able to represent spirit communing with spirit. It is this that makes one feel that Maupassant in comparison is obvious and vulgar. The strange, the terrible thing is that, looking at man in their different ways, these two great writers, Maupassant and Chekov, saw eye to eye. One was content to look upon the flesh, while the other, more nobly and subtly, surveyed the spirit; but they agreed that life was tedious and insignificant and that men were base, unintelligent and pitiful.

Graham Greene, From *The Spectator* (1934), by permission of David Higham Associates

This comes very generously from a disciple of Maupassant, and Mr. Maugham's praise of his master is never exaggerated. "Maupassant's stories are good stories. The anecdote is interesting apart from the narration, so that it would secure attention if it were told over the dinner table; and that seems to me a very great merit indeed." The best of Mr. Maugham's stories too are anecdotes, the best are worthy of Maupassant, and his failure really to reach Maupassant's rank is partly his failure to stick to the anecdote. Too many of his short stories sprawl into the proper region of the novel. Take for example "The Pool," where the scene changes from the South Seas to Scotland and back to the South Seas, where the action covers years, and of which the subject is the marriage of white and half-caste. Nor did Maupassant's preference for the anecdote imply a method which Mr. Maugham finds only too necessary: the method of the "yarn," of the first person singular. He defends the convention ably in his preface, but in a collected volume the monotony of the method becomes apparent. One has only to remember how this convention of the first person was transformed by Conrad, to realize a strange limitation to Mr. Maugham's interest in his craft.

This air of being at ease in a Sion which he so candidly and rightly despises is rather pronounced in his defence of the popular magazines. As he explains in his preface, he came to the short story late in his career, he was already well known as a dramatist, and it is not surprising that his stories have always been welcomed by the magazines. His good fortune has blinded him to the demands which the popular magazine makes on its less famous writers. When he remarks: "It has never been known yet that a good writer was unable to write his best owing to the conditions under which alone he could gain a public for his work," he has been misled, I think, by his own success. Writers belonging to a less easily appreciated school than the anecdotal, who depend for their market on the intellectual magazine, are lucky if they can earn £20 by a short story, while the writer who fits the taste of the popular magazine may well earn £200. It is seldom that financial worry is a condition for the best work.

H. E. Bates

To the young writers of post-war England he [Conrad] had little to offer.

Nor, rather surprisingly, had Maugham. Maugham is at once an attractive and a rather disconcerting figure. Beginning as a writer with, as it were, no ear for words, Maugham had very early to choose a stylistic model which his own limitations would permit him to follow without embarrassment. To have chosen a pretentious, poetical, highly coloured writer would have been fatal. Maugham chose Maupassant, and throughout his career has stuck to Maupassant. It is interesting to recall here that Maupassant has been described as "the born popular writer, battered by Flaubert into austerity," and perhaps Maugham is an example of the sort of writer, popular, cosmopolitan, commercial and yet in some way distinguished, that Maupassant might have been if left alone. Maugham is now, at his best, as in *Cakes and Ale*, a master of cultivated acidity. The spare sere detachment of his prose may, with the exception of recurrent lapses into appalling sentimentality, be safely offered as a sound foundation course in commercial-literary craftsmanship.

One other influence, not I believe admitted by Maugham, seems to have shaped his craft. Repeatedly throughout his work, speaking both for himself and through his characters, Maugham reveals an ironic impatience with the stuffiness of literary and moral conventions (see the delicious dissection of the pompous social-climbing novelist in *Cakes and Ale*), and is constantly administering the acid corrective. The parallel for this side of Maugham's method is not Maupassant, but *The Way of All Flesh*, a book for which Maugham is admirably fitted to write a modern counterpart. Here are two quotations:

> Like other rich men at the beginning of this century he ate and drank a good deal more than was enough to keep him in health. Even his excellent constitution was not proof against a prolonged course of overfeeding and what we should now consider overdrinking. His liver would not unfrequently get out of order, and he would come down to breakfast looking yellow about the eyes.

I fancy that life is more amusing now than it was forty years ago and I have a notion that people are more amiable. They may have been worthier then, possessed of more substantial knowledge; I do not know. I know they were more cantankerous; they ate too much, many of them drank too much, and they took too little exercise. Their livers were out of order and their digestions often impaired.

The account of the first paragraph, which is Butler, is pitched in a key identical with that of the second, which is Maugham. The effect in both is gained by a series of apparently matter-of-fact statements, made almost offhand, with a sort of casual formality, qualified by a sort of airy, "Of course I don't really know. Don't go and take my word for it," which in reality injects the note of irony. Maugham and Butler again and again use this trick of creating ironic effect by disclaiming all trustworthy knowledge of what they are talking about, and by pitching their remarks in a negative key. The effect is delicious; butter won't melt in these acid mouths. *The Way of All Flesh* and *Cakes and Ale* will, in fact, repay some pretty close comparative study, and will show, I think, that Maugham found a far more profitable and compatible influence in Butler than in Maupassant.

It is my contention in fact that if Maugham had, as a writer of stories, rejected Maupassant as a model and kept more closely to Butler, we should have been presented with the first full-length English short-story writer worthy of comparison with the best continental figures. Unfortunately Maugham, in spite of an excellent eye, a dispassionate steadiness, a genius for the diagnosis of human frailty, and a cosmopolitan temperament, lacks one very great and supremely important quality. Unlike Tchehov and Maupassant, in whom he professes to see great differences but who were much alike at least in this respect, Maugham lacks compassion. He has no heart, and in place of that heart one has the impression that he uses a piece of clockwork. It is this, I think, that gives Maugham's work the frequent impression of cheapness. This effect is heightened by something else. Maugham, having mastered the art of irony, mistakenly supposed himself to be a cynic. But throughout Maugham's work, and notably in the stories, there exists a pile of evidence to show that Maugham the cynic is in reality a tin-foil wrapping for Maugham the sentimentalist. Maugham's cynicism indeed peels off under too-close examination, thin, extraneous, tinny, revealing underneath a man who is afraid of trusting and finally of revealing his true emotions.

There would be little point, here, in doing more than summarize the

quality of Maugham's stories. They are easily available, pleasantly readable; they tell a story—in the sense, that is, that what they have to say can be expressed anecdotally; they deal largely with romantic places, for Maugham, like Kipling and Conrad, loves the East, and to his talent for painting its scenery and people he owes, as they do, much of his popular success. He delights in exposing human frailty, particularly amorous and marital frailty, and the humbug of convention; he is suave and urbane; he has the keenest sense of dramatic situations and delights in leaving the reader, as Maupassant and O. Henry did, with the point of the story neatly sharpened and vinegared in his hands. His natural sense of poetry is nil; his methods are as objective as the newspaper report of a court case, and sometimes as bad; he wisely refrains, except on rare occasions, from the purple passage, yet he has apparently never discovered any conscious and simple method of detecting himself in the act of using a cliché. When he is good, like the little girl, he is very good; and similarly when he is bad he is horrid.

Maugham indeed, though presenting the interesting case of a man who (on his own confession) evolved an attractively individual style without the help of a natural ear for words, has nothing new to offer. He simply perpetuates a tradition of straightforward, objective story-telling, largely derived from French naturalism, that is already well known. Thus Maugham's influence is not, and never has been, wide or important.

It is precisely for this reason that he is included, with Conrad, in a chapter designed primarily to show something of the first influences that were shaping the post–Great War short story. Neither Conrad nor Maugham, for all their popularity and excellence, contributed any lasting momentum to the short story's progress. The same may be said of their contemporaries. Galsworthy and Bennett, maintaining in their best work a sound tradition of realistic craftsmanship that should not (in Bennett especially) be underestimated, also wrote stories; so did W. H. Hudson (the volume *El Ombú* is excellent); so did many other well-known and well-liked writers of the day. But none threatened the orderly business of that day, as Joyce did, with a charge of dynamite; or the complacent patient, as Lawrence did, with a hypodermic injection of disturbing virulence. Conrad, Maugham, Bennett, Galsworthy, Hudson, and the many writers of their generation simply carried over into the new world the cooled and now unmalleable traditions of the old. For them it was too late to change; it was too late to be revolutionary. They left the art of the novel in general on a higher shelf than they had first found it: little more. The most important influences on the short story were to come, as always, from abroad.

Angus Wilson

Somerset Maugham wrote at one time or another more than one hundred short stories. Some are masterly; none is less than highly competent. To select a dozen of these is inevitably to mix critical judgement with personal taste. All the stories in this book are first class, but another editor might have replaced half of them with other stories of Maugham and yet not have lowered the standard of the whole book.

I make no defence for this personal choice except in one particular. Half the stories in this book are set in Malaysia or relate to that part of the world; two more are set in the South Seas. Some of Maugham's admirers may think that this choice gives a disproportionately narrow picture of the master's wide interests and knowledge of the world. What of his ironic vision of the Anglo-Saxons in the Mediterranean world? I have, in fact, included two stories of this area—one pure comedy, "The Three Fat Women of Antibes"; the other, "The Lotus Eater," one of the most moving and forbidding of the author's works in his occasional moods of stern morality. What of the comedy of the London and Home Counties scene in the years from 1914 to 1930? It is here that I plead guilty to omission. Such glimpses of England as the reader will get from this selection are oblique: London seen as the unfamiliar, scaring "home" of the English men and women on occasional leaves from Malaysia—in, for example, "Before the Party" and "Virtue." I believe this gives a more exact and a more just picture of Maugham's essential and remarkable contribution to the literature of human comedy.

From "Of Human Bondage" onwards, Maugham was essentially a lonely writer, an observer of life with a keen eye and a sharp ear, and, above all, an extraordinary sense of the hidden loneliness in others. This isolation is the source both of his exceptional powers and his limitations. It makes him a master of irony and compassion, but it cuts him off from the more fundamental sources of love and passion; it tempers his admiration for courage with an equal belief in prudence as we may see in "The Lotus Eater"; it makes him compassionate with the rebel but it

tempers that compassion with distrust of the heart as a guide to life as we can see in "Virtue"; but equally as we may see in "Footprints in the Jungle" he has little belief that the conventions and laws of society are an adequate measure of human worth. A sort of gregarious solitude as of a man always the silent fourth at bridge, the observer at the edge of a cocktail party, or the careful withdrawn host at dinner marks him and gives his work a wonderful poise and accuracy and loving care, but mars it at times with those pretences and defences with which lonely men in society always surround themselves. He can be ungraciously malicious where he feels unsure of himself; he is charged often with a superficial cynicism, but perhaps it is more important that this cynicism, as so often with lonely people, topples on the edge of sentimentality as we may see in his treatment of the surly odious Walker in "Mackintosh." This basic insecurity makes him, I think, at his most superficial when confronted with the clever, sophisticated world of London from which he was so often a self-imposed exile; in compensation it makes him the peculiar confidant and loving confessor of all those ordinary, tongue-tied, convention-bound exiles who once ruled and traded in the British Empire in Asia. At home as he was in the whole world of European smart society it seems absurd to class him with the young District Officer in "Virtue," Morton from Malay, who is lost amid Piccadilly's bright lights when home on leave, or with the most lovable of Maugham characters, Mrs. Hamlyn in "P. & O." who needs the mystery of death to awaken her heart as she returns from Japan in frozen loneliness to a London that means nothing to her; yet basically it is, I believe, with exiles that his place lay and about whom he wrote most feelingly. For this reason I have preferred to omit the well-known witty stories of London social or literary life like "Jane" or "The Creative Impulse"; their wit, I think, too shallowly covers the resentment of the outsider. Exile on the other hand awakens his love as in "P. & O.," his compassion as in "Footprints in the Jungle," and, best of all, his tragic acceptance as in "The Force of Circumstance."

No author, I suppose, has more cleverly converted his defects into assets, not only by his assumption of the classic and stoic framework of life through which the lost romantic is only occasionally allowed yearningly to peer, but far more by the perfection of his craft, imposing upon his carefully limited material an even more rigorous form, and then becoming so completely master of this highly artificial technique that his stories appear to flow with the ease and simplicity of ordinary, everyday muddled life. The discipline is so beautiful that he has rightly become the model in English of the "classic" form of short story, so that however

those of us who practise this craft may try to diverge into greater impressionism, more immediacy or whatever else we may feel "truer to life," we have always to measure our achievements against the rigorous perfection of form he has handed down to us. The appearance of simplicity, of course, is his masterly deception. His sentences, his prose have simplicity, the simplicity of rigorous pruning; but the form of his narratives is extraordinarily complex and any simplicity they appear to offer is a careful result of art. The narrator—frequently an "I" figure, any resemblance of which to himself Maugham always artfully denied—is in control, but within his narrative how dexterously and nimbly the story moves from mouth to mouth, from viewpoint to viewpoint, and backwards and forwards in time. It is by these alternations that Maugham achieves all his effects of irony, of pathos and of knowledge of life, the more apparently certain because it is handed out to us, the readers, so casually. Consider for a moment the narration of "Before the Party": we are in full middle-class suburbia whose narrowness and hypocrisy the author wishes to expose. Mrs. Skinner is wearing the ospreys sent to her by her late son-in-law from Malaya. The family assembles in the hall, ready to leave for a garden party where they will meet the bishop. But now it seems that Kathleen, the youngest daughter, when playing golf, has heard a less happy story of her brother-in-law's death than the one her widowed sister Millicent had brought back from Malaya. Suicide? Really, says Mr. Skinner, the most orthodox of solicitors, I should have been told the truth. And then Millicent begins to tell the truth. Her story moves back and forth in time, with interjections from the family. Is it true, asks Kathleen, that he drank? Like a fish, his widow abruptly replies. The ospreys begin to make Mrs. Skinner distressed. And then the bereaved widow goes flatly on with her macabre story of D.T.s at a remote Malay station. And at last we know that it was neither a natural death nor drink nor suicide, for she tells how she murdered her husband. And then they must all go off, sharing her secret, to meet the bishop. They'll get used to it in time, she tells them. But Mr. Skinner in the car must point out that really as a respectable solicitor he should never have been told the truth.

It all seems so easy, and so do the other eleven in the book but they are the end result of the most complex and economic narration, which is totally successful in giving the appearance of reality and ease to what is in fact a complete subjection of life to the discipline of art. This artistic discipline and skill with words will surely earn the admiration of new and younger readers for whom the setting of Imperial exile will now have the additional fascination of historical curiosity.

Archie K. Loss

Very early in his career as a writer, Maugham published a volume of short fiction, but then, for nearly two decades, he abandoned the form, concentrating instead upon drama and longer fiction. In 1920, however, following a trip to the South Seas, he returned to it by writing a classic story—surely his most famous contribution to the genre—the often-anthologized "Rain," which became the basis of a popular play (not by Maugham) and also of a number of films. "Rain" is in many respects a paradigm for what Maugham was to do in the short-story form for the next thirty years or so. The work of a mature writer who knew what he was aiming at, it deserves a close examination for what it can tell about his short-story technique and subject matter.

Of the latter, the first thing that strikes us in "Rain" is the exotic locale, a setting that Maugham staked out early as his own. Other authors in England had written of colonial types in similar settings—Rudyard Kipling and Joseph Conrad come first to mind—but Maugham in his short stories focuses especially on the effect of an exotic environment upon marital (or extramarital) relationships. In his plays (for the most part comedies) Maugham focuses similarly on personal relationships, but generally not in exotic settings.[1] In the short stories, the subject of conjugal fidelity (or infidelity) is transferred from the drawing room to the tropical porch, with its bamboo furniture and ever-present native servants. E. M. Forster once said that Sinclair Lewis, with his American characters, had managed "to lodge a piece of a continent in our imagination"[2]; Maugham, with characters who are predominantly English colonials, manages to do almost the same in his short fiction, set primarily in the East. The key element of the characters in "Rain" and elsewhere in the early stories is less than Englishness, however, than the sense of exile that they convey. Three of the major characters in "Rain" are in fact American, but all of the characters, whether American, English, or European, are in some way exiled from their native land.

For the Davidsons, as well as for the MacPhails, exile is a matter of choice. For Miss Sadie Thompson, it is a matter of necessity. In no case, however, is anyone in his or her native environment. Maugham writes many stories with an English setting, and many of them are among his finest achievements in the form. However, it is for the exotic setting that he is best known, and it is on the whole in stories like these that he had his greatest success as a writer of short fiction. If we consider Maugham's personal relationship to the English environment, his interest in the exiled is not difficult to understand.

In "Rain," there is on the one hand the grimly puritanical Reverend Davidson and his wife, for only the latter of whom one might feel the slightest degree of sympathy by the end of the story. On the other, there is the slatternly Sadie Thompson, whose attempt at greater moral perfection leads to an even greater imperfection of personal appearance and who ends up no more appealing a character than she was at the beginning, in spite of the unpleasant experience to which she has been subjected and the sympathy it creates for her in the reader. In the final analysis, Sadie is not the whore with a golden heart of popular fiction, nor is she a type of the adulteress Christ encounters at the well and to whom the reverend refers in the story. She is exactly what she is, and what she learns is that the Reverend Davidson is exactly like all the other men she has ever known.

Between these characters (both in the physical and the moral sense) comes the important character of Doctor MacPhail. MacPhail serves as the buffer between the Reverend Davidson's overbearing self-righteousness and Sadie Thompson's crumbling, highly vulnerable sense of self. He is described more than once in the story as "timid" or unable to take a firm stand, but when push comes to shove he goes to the governor's office on the behalf of Sadie Thompson. His sympathies go increasingly to her as Reverend Davidson's attempts at her reformation persist. "Live and let live," is Doctor MacPhail's motto; he does not like to be put in the position of having to judge the behavior, moral or otherwise, of other people, but, all the same, he clearly does not side with Reverend Davidson and what he represents.

It is significant in regard to this prevailingly neutral attitude that MacPhail is a physician, for his attitude toward human behavior is much the same as a physician's attitude toward his patients: he notes their behavior, for the most part without passing judgment on it. In other words, he takes the same attitude already noted in Maugham as an author and in the first-person narrators who serve as Maugham's personae in his longer fiction. Doctor MacPhail corresponds to these dispassionate commentators on the human condition.[3] Like them, MacPhail serves to bring the other characters of the story into focus for the reader. It is *through* him that one finds out what Reverend Davidson is hoping to accomplish with Sadie Thompson—or, more properly, through his conversations with Horn or with Davidson or with Sadie herself—not by direct access to the prayer sessions they hold. No major incident of the story is rendered directly for the reader.

This indirect approach, one might argue, is essential to the point of Maugham's story. If one knew precisely what was going on between Sadie and Davidson—in particular what emotions Davidson felt—there would be no surprise at the end. As it is, the reader is given more than a sufficient number of clues that the story will end as it does, beginning with the reference early on to the reverend's "suppressed fire" and "full" and "sensual lips," but these clues come primarily from what others say about the principals and from how Doctor MacPhail reacts to what they say, not from the principals themselves.

Doctor MacPhail thus serves an essential purpose as the character who, by what he observes more than by what he says, brings the behavior of the other characters into focus, both in terms of the plot and of the theme. His place in other Maugham stories may be taken by the narrator through whom characters and events are seen, but, whatever the person, it is more typical of Maugham to tell a story indirectly than to tell it through the unmediated actions of its main characters. In this, "Rain" conforms to the narrative strategy typical of most of Maugham's short stories.

It also conforms to the structure of the typical Maugham story. In his novels Maugham tends at times toward a loose structure, but in his short stories, as in his work for the theater, he follows the classic pattern of the short tale that tends toward a single effect, defined so well in the nineteenth century by Edgar Allan Poe.[4] Without too much distortion, the elements of the classic tale, including turning point and climax, can be perceived in "Rain," though the result of applying such terms to it is to tell only what is already known: that the author builds his story toward Sadie Thompson's final line and the suicide that immediately precedes it. The plot structure of the story thus consists of a series of items of withheld information that can be rendered as questions—why does Sadie not want to return to San Francisco? why is Reverend Davidson so eager to reform her?—and the curve of the plot begins its inevitable descent at that point in the story when Reverend Davidson resolves to break Sadie's will. All else follows in the wake of that ominous decision.

At its best, as in "Rain," this sort of action has a sense of inevitability to it; at its worst, it is merely slick. Seldom, however, is Maugham content simply to sketch a character and not provide a plot by which that character can demonstrate his or her potential for good or evil. Even the most trivial of his stories builds toward some final line or action. The stories end emphatically, and the sense of character they convey is fixed: our initial impression of a character is usually borne out by his or her subsequent behavior. If bad, they may grow slightly worse, but they seldom become better; if good—though their goodness may lead them to folly—they are likely not to turn evil. Good may come of evil actions, or evil of good, but the moral nature of the characters tends to be of a piece.

The cynic always tends to view human nature as fixed, and this perhaps accounts for the feeling one gets in Maugham's best short fiction (as in his long) that his characters are simply fulfilling our expectations of them. In the course of his long career as a writer of short fiction, Maugham varies his subject matter, but seldom his themes, his technique, or his fundamental sense of human nature. The ground might shift to England or to the south of France, but with great consistency the themes remain the selfishness of human motives and the frailty of human will.

For all this consistency of theme, Maugham's stories derive from a variety of sources. The main purpose of most of his travels was to find material to write about. The stories about British colonials in the Far East began after Maugham's first trip there, and all of his subsequent journeys throughout the world produced their own material. Some stories show almost a reportorial approach to their subject matter, as, for instance, "The Letter," which appeared in a collection of 1926 and which sticks very close to the details of a celebrated murder trial in Kuala Lumpur of some twenty-five years earlier.[5]

If the real-life sources of Maugham's subject matter lay in various and sundry places, his literary sources are easier to trace. For his technique of telling a story, Maugham's great model from beginning to end is Guy de Maupassant:

> From the age of fifteen whenever I went to Paris I spent most of my afternoons poring over the books in the galleries of the Odeon. I have never passed more enchanted hours. The attendants in their long

smocks were indifferent to the people who sauntered about looking at the books and they would let you read for hours without bothering. There was a shelf filled with the works of Guy de Maupassant, but they cost three francs fifty a volume and that was not a sum I was prepared to spend. I had to read as best I could standing up and peering between the uncut pages. Sometimes when no attendant was looking I would hastily cut a page and thus read more conveniently. Fortunately some of them were issued in a cheap edition at seventy-five centimes and I seldom came away without one of these. In this manner, before I was eighteen, I had read all the best stories. It is natural enough that when at that age I began writing stories myself I should unconsciously have chosen those little masterpieces as a model. I might very well have hit upon a worse.

Thus Maugham wrote of his first encounter with the work of the nineteenth-century French master.[6] In contrast with Maupassant, he goes on in the same preface, is the work of Anton Chekhov (and one might add, by extension, many masters of the early twentieth-century short story). Such work emphasizes not action, but character or atmosphere; in contrast with Maugham's ideal short story, little happens in it. Maugham clearly favors the technique of Maupassant, in spite of his clear admiration for Chekhov's gifts.

A second important literary source for Maugham's short fiction is Poe. In one of his last literary essays Maugham described what Poe's concept of the short story meant to him:

It is a piece of fiction, dealing with a single incident, material or spiritual, that can be read at a sitting; it is original, it must sparkle, excite or impress; and it must have unity of effect or impression. It should move in an even line from its exposition to its close. To write a story on the principles he laid down is not so easy as some think.[7]

If the effect of some of Maugham's tales is less concentrated than some of his pronouncements suggest, one cannot impugn his intention to achieve the desired single effect.

In short fiction as in long, Maugham's technique—especially in the first person—is that of teller of tales. This approach allows him a high degree of narrative flexibility. He can move at will from character to character, shifting view-point as he pleases. He can even make use of one or more tellers before getting to the heart of his story. Furthermore, he can do all of this without narrative tone except as the conversation of his characters dictates. If he does not provide a story made aesthetically consistent by its portrayal of the consciousness of a single character (in the manner of Henry James or James Joyce), he does achieve unity through the *tone* in which each story is told. The voice of the narrator, whether in first person or third (or occasionally second, as in one paragraph in "Rain"), thus becomes the most important single unifying element in a Maugham short story.[8]

Atmosphere is another important unifying element. I noted earlier the exotic locale of "Rain." In virtually all of the stories set in the East, descriptive details are important in establishing both mood and character. "Rain" itself provides an obvious example with the physical circumstance suggested by the title. The repeated references to the rain pouring down in the steamy tropical climate add to the sense of imminence created by the small events of the story. Like the celebrated drums constantly in the background in Eugene O'Neill's play *The Emperor Jones* (1920), Maugham's rain suggests the lack of will and obsessiveness often associated with the tropical environment.

Among modern British short stories, Maugham's work stands in the conservative side of a generally conservative lot. Authors like Katherine Mansfield or Virginia Woolf or D. H. Lawrence, whose work was considered innovative when it first appeared, were innovative chiefly in terms of their subject matter or themes. In comparison, continental authors were abandoning traditional forms of short fiction altogether in favor of new, polygeneric forms that fused fiction, poetry, and drama into one.[9] Mainstream twentieth-century British short fiction, as practiced by later writers such as L. P. Hartley, H. E. Bates, or V. S. Pritchett, was neither experimental nor innovative; it is well-crafted work that deals with closely observed patterns of human behavior, with occasional insights gleaned from psychology or myth. Maugham's work, which was essentially nineteenth-century in form, lay somewhat to the right of this solid center. In the end, Maugham's work is closer to that of earlier authors like Rudyard Kipling or Poe—not to mention Maupassant—than it is to the work of most of his contemporaries.

One group of stories in the Maugham canon deserves particular mention—the group, including the celebrated "Mr. Harrington's Washing," collected under the title *Ashenden* (1928). In this volume Maugham brought to fictional life his experiences as a British agent during World War I. Together, these stories achieve sufficient unity of tone and purpose to amount nearly to a novel.[10]

Their central character is the precise opposite of the conventional image of the spy. That image—nurtured in fiction of this period and before by such popular authors as E. Phillips Oppenheim, Anthony Hope, and Ouida—required the spy to be a dashing, romantic figure: handsome, cosmopolitan, ready to do service to the ladies as readily as to his country, native or chosen. Such spies and adventurers were latter-day versions of the Count of Monte Cristo and predecessors to Ian Fleming's popular James Bond.

The Ashenden of Maugham's stories, on the other hand, is reserved, stoic, unromantic; his work is dull, repetitive, even meaningless. He seems to have been chosen for his task because, whatever talent he may have as a writer, he does not know much about espionage and is not likely to wish to distinguish himself by unusually courageous and possibly foolish behavior. He is, in short, more acted upon then active; he lets events (or superiors) dictate his moves rather than attempt to dictate events for himself; and he deliberately avoids romantic contacts the result of which might be the vitiation of his responsibilities. He is the unheroic hero—not a hero at all, but an observer, chosen for his task because of his powers of observation and his distance from others. He is soon to reappear in fiction in the spy novels of Graham Greene and, much later, in the novels of John le Carré.[11]

In Maugham's body of work, Ashenden is remarkable for his contribution to the development of the persona that I have already noted in the longer fiction and that I have suggested came partly as a result of Maugham's desire to distance himself from his alter ego in *Of Human Bondage.* Unheroic or unromantic though he may be, Ashenden is at least not the victim of a self-willed persecution, the slave of emotions that lead him to increasingly neurotic behavior. He is, if anything, above emotions, so that one tends (as with Doctor MacPhail in "Rain") to see events through him. He suggests a dimension of character distinctly different from Philip Carey's, and his next major manifestation—in *Cakes and Ale*—sees him broadened further still.

One of the best features of *Ashenden* (as in much of the short fiction) is its understated style, and one of the best examples of that style comes in the final story of the group, as Anastasia Alexandrovna leads Ashenden to Mr. Harrington's body in revolutionary Russia:

> Anastasia Alexandrovna touched Ashenden's arm to draw his attention: sitting on the pavement, her head bent right down to her lap, was a woman and she was dead. A little way on two men had fallen

together. They were dead too. The wounded, one supposed, had managed to drag themselves away or their friends had carried them. Then they found Mr. Harrington. His derby had rolled in the gutter. He lay on his face, in a pool of blood, his bald head, with its prominent bones, very white; his neat black coat smeared and muddy. But his hand was clenched tight on the parcel that contained four shirts, two union suits, a pair of pyjamas and four collars. Mr. Harrington had not let his washing go.

The prose in this passage has both tautness and immediacy, and the final line (typical of a Maugham story) provides a satisfying touch. If one is fond of this kind of fiction, one ends by wishing that Maugham had decided to come back to it again.

In the end, the Ashenden stories notwithstanding, one probably remembers best the Maugham short stories that, like "Rain," have exotic settings. These stories continue the account of the British imperial experience begun by Kipling, carrying it into its decadence and ultimate corruption, the last to be memorialized in fiction much later on by writers like Paul Scott (in his *Raj Quartet*). Maugham's short stories also continue the tradition of the nineteenth-century tale. "No author," Angus Wilson observed of Maugham in a preface to a selection of his short stories, "has more cleverly converted his defects into assets, not only by his assumption of the classic and stoic framework of life (through which the lost romantic is only occasionally allowed yearningly to peer), but far more by the perfection of his craft, imposing upon his carefully limited material an even more rigorous form, and then becoming so completely master of this highly artificial technique that his stories appear to flow with the ease and simplicity of ordinary, everyday muddled life."[12] In the best of the short fiction, through such means, Maugham achieved a vision and tone uniquely his. If he had written nothing else, his best short stories would guarantee him a place of note in English literary history.

Notes

1. An exception is *East of Suez*, a melodrama written and produced in 1922.
2. "Sinclair Lewis," in *Abinger Harvest* (New York: Meridian Books, 1955), p. 123.
3. It is in fact possible, especially in the early pages of this story, to substitute first-person for third-person references to Doctor MacPhail and in no way do any disservice to our sense of the story or to MacPhail's part in it. Here, for instance, is the opening passage, with the changes indicated in italics;

It was nearly bed-time and when *we* awoke next morning land would be in sight. *I* lit *my* pipe and, leaning over the rail, searched the heavens for the Southern Cross. After two years at the front and a wound that had taken longer to heal than it should, *I* was glad to settle down quietly at Apia for twelve months at least, and *I* felt already better for the journey.

This is in many respects a typical opening to a first-person Maugham story.

4. See for example Poe's review of "Hawthorne's Tales," reprinted in *The Shock of Recognition: The Development of Literature in the United States Recorded by the Men Who Made It* (New York: Farrar, Straus and Cudahy, 1955), edited by Edmund Wilson, especially pp. 162–65. From such reviews Poe's principles of fiction are to be inferred. The development of the short story, as Poe was well aware, was linked to the development of the large-circulation magazines that published them.

5. Morgan, pp. 252–53. In "Changing Views of Empire: The Imperial Themes of Somerset Maugham," *Research Studies* (Washington State University), 47 (September 1979), pp. 145–53, Kathryne S. McDorman deals generally with the treatment of the British empire in Maugham's work, comparing the prewar and postwar views.

6. Preface to *The Complete Short Stories*, vol. 1 (*East and West*) (Garden City, NY: Doubleday, 1934), p. vii.

7. "The Short Story," in *Points of View* (London: Heinemann, 1958), p. 155.

8. Maugham saw the device of the first-person narrator limiting his range in storytelling: "It makes it possible for the writer to tell no more than he knows. Making no claim to omniscience, he can frankly say when a motive or an occurrence is unknown to him, and thus often give his story a plausibility that it might otherwise lack. It tends also to put the reader on intimate terms with the author" (preface to *Complete Short Stories*, vol. 1, p. xv). This last comment leads to the observation of John Brophy: "He is less a writer than a talker—a view of him which is supported by the character of his prose and the construction of his novels and stories, and which is consonant with his success in the necessarily oral conventions of the theatre and cinema" (*Somerset Maugham*, p. 25). The second-person paragraph in "Rain" is the one beginning "Iwelei was on the edge of the city."

9. As in the work of the Italian futurists, which preceded the First World War by five years or more. For the theoretical basis for such polygeneric work, later of significance to the surrealists, see F. T. Marinetti, *Selected Writings* (New York: Farrar, Straus and Giroux, 1972). Needless to say, such experimentalism was anathema to Maugham.

10. For background on Maugham in Russia, see Rhodri Jeffreys-Jones, "W. Somerset Maugham: Anglo-American Agent in Revolutionary Russia," *American Quarterly* 28 (1979), pp. 90–106. Morgan also provides an account, pp. 226–32.

11. Indeed, Maugham, with the character of Ashenden the spy, may be said to have begun a tradition that remains very much alive. It is much as if Dr. Watson, not Sherlock Holmes, were the main character in the stories by Arthur Conan Doyle. But Ashenden is in no sense a bungler or a fool; it is his job that is unexceptional, not himself.

12. Introduction to *Cakes and Ale and Twelve Short Stories*, selected by Angus Wilson (Garden City, NY: Doubleday, 1967), p. 7.

Chronology

1874   William Somerset Maugham born at the British embassy, Paris, on 25 January, fourth son of a British solicitor and his socialite wife.

1882   Mother dies.

1884   Father dies. Maugham, age 10, sent from France to Whitstable, England, to live with his uncle, the Reverend Henry Macdonald Maugham and his German-born wife, Sophie.

1885   Enters King's School, Canterbury.

1890–1891   Travels to Germany, where he spends more than a year at Heidelberg.

1892   Enters medical school at St. Thomas's Hospital, London, completing his medical studies in 1897. At age 18 writes his first two short stories, "Daisy" and "A Sad Case."

1897   *Liza of Lambeth*, his first novel, published.

1898   Travels to Spain; first published story, "Don Sebastian," appears in the obscure magazine *Cosmopolis* in October.

1899   *Orientations*, first volume of short stories, includes six early stories.

1899–1909   Continues a varied literary career, finding little success in novels, travel literature, and dramas. Fifteen short stories published in periodicals. *Lady Frederick* (1907) launches his career as a successful dramatist.

1914–1915   Serves as ambulance driver in France during World War I.

1915   *Of Human Bondage*, an autobiographical novel, published. Becomes an agent for British Military Intelligence in Switzerland.

1916   Travels to Hawaii and Samoa with Gerald Haxton, his American secretary, gathering material for the South Sea stories.

1917   Serves as intelligence agent in Russia. Gathers material for the *Ashenden* stories. Marries Syrie Bernardo Wellcome.

1919   *The Moon and Sixpence*, a novel based on the life of Paul Gauguin, published. Composes "Rain," his first South Sea story.

1921   *The Trembling of a Leaf*, containing six stories of the South Seas, published.

1922   *On a Chinese Screen*, travel literature containing sketches and stories, published.

1926   *The Casuarina Tree*, six additional South Sea stories, published. Purchases the Villa Mauresque on the French Riviera, his residence for the remainder of his life.

1927   *The Letter*, a drama adapted from a short story, produced and published. Syrie Maugham files for divorce.

1928   *Ashenden*, a collection of spy fiction.

1929   The Maughams are divorced.

1930   *The Gentleman in the Parlour*, travel volume containing stories and sketches, published.

1931   *Six Stories Written in the First Person Singular*, published.

1933   Publication of *Ah King: Six Stories*, his third and final volume of South Sea stories, and *Traveller's Library*, an anthology containing notes on the art of fiction.

1934   Publication of *Altogether*, collected edition of 30 stories (published as *East and West* in the United States).

1936   *Cosmopolitans* published.

1938   *The Summing Up*, an autobiography containing extended observations on the art of fiction.

1939   *Tellers of Tales*, an anthology of 100 short stories, published; includes his extended preface on the storyteller's art.

1940   *The Mixture as Before*, a collection of stories, published.

1945   Writes "The Colonel's Lady," his last short story.

1947   *Creatures of Circumstance*, his final collection of stories, published.

1949   *A Writer's Notebook*, including his observations on the story as form and offering material on his sources, published.

1951   *Complete Short Stories* published in three volumes by William Heinemann.

1965   Dies on 19 December at the Villa Mauresque, his home near Nice, France.

1969   *Seventeen Lost Stories*, a collection of stories Maugham omitted from the complete edition, published.

1984   *A Traveller in Romance*, including four additional stories omitted from earlier collections.

Selected Bibliography

Primary Works

Editions

Ah King. London: William Heinemann, 1933.
Ashenden; or, The British Agent. London: William Heinemann, 1928.
The Casuarina Tree. London: William Heinemann, 1926.
Cosmopolitans. Garden City, N.Y.: Doubleday, Doran, 1936.
Creatures of Circumstance. London: William Heinemann, 1947.
The Mixture as Before. London: William Heinemann, 1940.
Orientations. London: T. Fisher Unwin, 1899.
Six Stories Written in the First Person Singular. Garden City, N.Y.: Doubleday, Doran, 1931.
The Trembling of a Leaf. New York: George H. Doran, 1921.

Collected Editions

The Complete Short Stories of W. Somerset Maugham. 3 vols. London: William Heinemann, 1951.
The Complete Short Stories of W. Somerset Maugham. 2 vols. Garden City, N.Y.: Doubleday, 1952.

Criticism and Travel Literature

The Gentleman in the Parlour. London: William Heinemann, 1930.
Great Modern Reading: W. Somerset Maugham's Introduction to Modern English and American Literature. Garden City, N.Y.: Doubleday, 1943.
Maugham's Choice of Kipling's Best. Garden City, N.Y.: Doubleday, 1953.
On a Chinese Screen. New York: George H. Doran, 1922.
Points of View. London: William Heinemann, 1958.
Selected Prefaces and Introductions of W. Somerset Maugham. Garden City, N.Y.: Doubleday, 1963.
The Summing Up. London: William Heinemann, 1938.
Tellers of Tales. New York: Doubleday, Doran, 1939.
The Traveller's Library. Garden City, N.Y.: Doubleday, Doran, 1933.
A Writer's Notebook. London: William Heinemann, 1949.

Selected Editions

A Baker's Dozen. London: William Heinemann, 1970.

The Best Short Stories of W. Somerset Maugham. Selected and with an introduction by John Beecroft. New York: Modern Library, 1957.

Encore. London: William Heinemann, 1951.

The Favourite Short Stories of W. Somerset Maugham. Garden City, N. Y.: Doubleday, Doran, 1937.

A Maugham Twelve. Selected and with an introduction by Angus Wilson. London: William Heinemann, 1966.

Quartet. London: William Heinemann, 1948.

A Second Baker's Dozen. London: William Heinemann, 1970.

Selected Stories. Illustrated by Guy Deel. Franklin Center, Pa.: Franklin Library, 1979.

Seventeen Lost Stories by W. Somerset Maugham. Compiled and with an introduction by Craig V. Showalter. Garden City, N.Y.: Doubleday, 1969.

Sixty-five Short Stories. New York: William Heinemann and Octopus Books, 1979.

30 Great Short Stories. New York: Doubleday, 1984.

A Traveller in Romance: Uncollected Writings, 1901–1964. Edited by John Whitehead. New York: Clarkson N. Potter, 1984.

Trio. London: William Heinemann, 1950.

Secondary Works

Bibliography

Sanders, Charles. *W. Somerset Maugham: An Annotated Bibliography of Writings about Him.* DeKalb: Northern Illinois University Press, 1970.

Stott, Raymond Toole. *A Bibliography of the Works of W. Somerset Maugham.* Rev. ed. London: Kaye & Ward, 1973.

Biography and Criticism

Bates, H. E. *The Modern Short Story: A Critical Survey.* Boston: The Writer, 1972.

Brander, L. *Somerset Maugham: A Guide.* New York: Barnes & Noble, 1963.

Brophy, John. *Somerset Maugham.* London: Longmans, Green, 1958.

Burt, Forrest D. *W. Somerset Maugham.* Boston: Twayne Publishers, 1985.

Calder, Robert Lorin. *W. Somerset Maugham and the Quest for Freedom.* Garden City, N.Y.: Doubleday, 1973.

———.*Willie: The Life of W. Somerset Maugham.* New York: St. Martin's Press, 1989.

Cordell, Richard A. *Somerset Maugham: A Biographical and Critical Study.* Bloomington: Indiana University Press, 1969.

Selected Bibliography

Curtis, Anthony. *The Pattern of Maugham*. London: Hamish Hamilton, 1974.
———, and Whitehead, John, eds. *W. Somerset Maugham: The Critical Heritage*. London and New York: Routledge & Kegan Paul, 1987.
Dobrinsky, Joseph. *La jeunesse de Somerset Maugham (1874–1903)*. Paris: Didier, 1976.
Kanin, Garson. *Remembering Mr. Maugham*. New York: Atheneum, 1966.
Loss, Archie K. *W. Somerset Maugham*. New York: Ungar, 1987.
MacCarthy, Desmond. *William Somerset Maugham: "The English Maupassant."* London: William Heinemann, 1934.
Menard, Wilmon. *The Two Worlds of Somerset Maugham*. Los Angeles: Sherbourne Press, 1965.
Morgan, Ted. *Maugham*. New York: Simon & Schuster, 1980.
Whitehead, John. *Maugham: A Reappraisal*. London: Vision Press, 1987.

Articles

Bedell, Jeanne F. "Somerset Maugham's *Ashenden* and the Modernization of Espionage Fiction." *Studies in Popular Culture* 7 (Winter, 1984): 40–46.
Belloc, Elizabeth. "The Stories of Somerset Maugham." *Month*, July–August 1964, 67–72.
Judson, Abe. "Love and Death in the Short Stories of W. Somerset Maugham: A Psychological Analysis." *Psychiatric Quarterly* 37 (Spring, 1963):250–62.
Mortimer, Armine K. "Second Stories: The Example of 'Mr. Know-All.'" *Studies in Short Fiction* 25 (Summer, 1988):307–14.
Pollock, John. "Somerset Maugham and His Work." *Quarterly Review* 304 (October, 1966):365–78.

Index

The Author

Stanley Archer is a professor in the Department of English at Texas A&M University. His publications, primarily on seventeenth-century English literature, have appeared in such journals as *ELH*, *Papers on Language and Literature*, *Milton Quarterly*, *Restoration and Eighteenth Century Theatre Research*, *Notes & Queries*, and *English Language Notes*. In addition, he is the author of *Richard Hooker* (Twayne Publishers, 1983). He has previously written reference articles on Maugham, and his paper on art in *Of Human Bondage* appeared in *English Literature in Transition*.

The Editor

General Editor Gordon Weaver earned his B.A. in English at the University of Wisconsin-Milwaukee in 1961; his M.A. in English at the University of Illinois, where he studied as a Woodrow Wilson Fellow, in 1962; and his Ph.D. in English and creative writing at the University of Denver in 1970. He is author of several novels, including *Count a Lonely Cadence, Give Him a Stone, Circling Byzantium*, and most recently *The Eight Corners of the World* (1988). Many of his numerous short stories are collected in *The Entombed Man of Thule, Such Waltzing Was Not Easy, Getting Serious, Morality Plan, A World Quite Round*, and *Men Who Would Be Good* (1991). Recognition of his fiction includes the St. Lawrence Award for Fiction (1973), two National Endowment for the Arts Fellowships (1974, 1989), and the O. Henry First Prize (1979). He edited *The American Short Story, 1945–1980: A Critical History*, and is currently editor of *Cimarron Review*. He is professor of English at Oklahoma State University. Married, and the father of three daughters, he lives in Stillwater, Oklahoma.